IN THE THOUGHT WORLD

ARVIND UPADHYAY

There is a fundamental law of attraction in the universe that guides people's lives and is the underlying power behind all things. This law was expressed by Napoleon Hill when he said, "We become what we think about." This profound truth has been stated in many different languages and cultures throughout history. In the second century of the Common Era, the Roman emperor and Stoic philosopher Marcus Aurelius said "Our life is what our thoughts make it." This idea has been developed over time and has now become a central tenet in many spiritual traditions. Its truth has spread to many people and has more recently been expressed in a popular quote: Watch your thoughts, for they become words. Watch your words, for they become actions. Watch your actions, for they become habits. Watch your habits, for they become character. Watch your character, for it becomes your destiny.

ARVIND UPADHYAY FROM THIS BOOK---

In relation to the law of attraction, we have extensive references to the idea of karma in the teachings of the Buddha. It is explained to us that our actions don't only have

an effect in this life but in future lives and that this is the reason for our own misfortunes right this minute. If we are to ever escape the endless cycles of misfortune, we will have to change our direction and achieve an end to our sorrows. If anyone says that a man or woman must reap in this life according to his present deeds, in that case there is no religious life, nor is an opportunity afforded for the entire extinction of sorrow. But if anyone says that what a man or woman reaps in this and future lives accords with his or her deeds present and past, in that case there is a religious life, and an opportunity is afforded for the entire extinction of a sorrow.2 – BUDDHA In the New Testament, Christians are very familiar with the phrase "As ye sow, so shall ye reap."3 This idea, presented to Christians and Buddhists alike, has also been presented in many other great religions on Earth and has been expounded by modern philosophers as well. Earl Nightengale has referred to the law of attraction as "The Strangest Secret". When asked by his readers, "Why do you call it the strangest secret?" he explains that it is a secret that is really "no secret" at all. It's not because the law of attraction is hidden from view that makes it so strange. In fact, it isn't hidden. It's extremely obvious and yet nobody seems to be aware of it. "We become what we think about" is no "secret" at all and that's what makes it so strange.

When we think about attraction, we often think about the person who makes us feel the best. We think about 'being attractive' or 'having an attraction'. Everyone knows about it because attraction is often associated with individual people who we wish to emulate or "become". These people are the ones who have all the 'right' qualities; they are beautiful, intelligent or possessing a great personality. They have all the things we want in ourselves. Attraction is a very powerful energy and yet it is often misunderstood in terms of its immense power. This is because we often limit our understanding to the manner in which we view other people. Scientists, however, say that the power of attraction is actually one of the four fundamental interactions in nature and goes much further than just a power between people. Attraction is a power in nature that can act over great distances. According to science and other great teachings, attraction is something that affects absolutely everything in the universe. When we look back over the history of science, we remember that Newton's law of gravitation first told us that every object in the universe was attracted by every other object. Einstein's theory also told us that attraction arose out of a space-time continuum. Einstein said that the attraction objects had for one another was actually their very reason for existence. The earth, the sun, and all the other celestial bodies would never have been formed if it weren't for the power of attraction.5 Even today, modern scientists still don't understand a lot of things about the power of attraction. Psychologists have studied these phenomena and have found them to be closely linked with the power of love but many aspects of these pow ers are still a mystery. With the help of Newton and Einstein, modern science has learned a lot but has still run up against a big problem in their understanding about attraction. LIMITS OF SCIENTIFIC UNDERSTANDING The problem about attraction, scientists say, is that the golden laws of Newton and Einstein only work well on our little old planet "Earth". The earlier theories that Newton and Einstein invented really don't explain the motion of the stars in their galaxies and the bending of light in our universe. In these vast galaxies, the laws that make sense on Earth really don't make sense in outer space. According to the laws of Newton and Einstein, it seems as though the stars should be thrown off in all directions! The whole universe shouldn't be functioning as well as it does and yet, something is holding it together. With this confusion in science, how do we explain the underlying order that has been maintained in our universe for billions of years? One solution to the scientific problem of attraction was proposed by another scientist named Fritz Zwicky in 1933.

Dr. Zwicky made a small step toward explaining attraction and the behavior of the stars when he proposed an 'unseen material' in the galaxies called 'dark matter'. Zwicky thought that dark matter would help to explain why the planets remained fixed in their orbits even when Newton and Einstein thought they should fly apart.6 Dark matter has done a lot of things to help explain the behavior of the stars but it has still left a lot of questions unanswered. It often seems that science may never be able to explain this mysterious power known as attraction even as it continues on its quest for knowledge.

The most beautiful thing we can experience is the mysterious. It is the source of all true art and all science. He to whom this emotion is a stranger, who can no longer pause to wonder and stand rapt in awe, is as good as dead: his eyes are closed.7 – ALBERT EINSTEIN The power of attraction is not only a great mystery in terms of the stars and planets but a great mystery in terms of people's lives. When two people come together, there is often an irresistible quality of attraction that overpowers every other desire they have. Because this power is so closely connected with the power of love, the attraction can even keep two people together forever. If we are able to understand the factors behind this amazing power that can keep two people together forever, we will have to look more deeply beyond science and reason. We will have to consult some of the great spiritual minds that can give us a deeper glance into the nature of both attraction and love. ATTRACTION AND LOVE The great spiritual teachers in history have always given us a solution to the problems that science and reason cannot seem to solve. Spiritual traditions have explained much more about the power of attraction by explaining to us more about a further power known as the power of love. This power that the spiritual teachers have spoken of is considered to be even stronger than the power of attraction because it has the potential to keep two people together for longer periods of time. When the simple power of attraction eventually fades, the power of love is there to sustain the relationship that otherwise would have ended. In science, objects may first be attracted to each other by the simple fact that they are different and share qualities in each other that bring about a balance. Eventually, however, these same objects may be attracted by other objects and the initial bond that was formed can be broken. The power which keeps objects together and may actually hold the enormous galaxies together may be similar to what we call love in human relationships. It may be a lot more than just the simple power of attraction and may be something that science will never understand. Love is the motivating power of the universe...The majesty of this realization cannot be over-emphasized. We need to realize it far more deeply and potently than we do, for it constitutes the basic, fundamental character and quality of all events, no matter what the outer appearance may be.8 – ALICE BAILEY Love is far from being the kind of explanation that science is looking for in our modern world. Still, this refusal to look at the larger picture may actually be the reason that science often sees the questions as part of a 'dark matter'. What is needed is a wider vision of reality that is reflective on the totality of things. Love is not something which can control or manipulate nature. It serves no useful function in scientific thought. Love is a completely different kind of energy that is not as easy to explain and yet, it leads us toward a greater vision of wholeness and oneness in nature.Reason deals only with particulars, whereas Love deals with entireties. This ability, often ascribed to intuition, is the capacity for instantaneous understanding without resorting to sequential symbolprocessing.9 – DR. DAVID R. HAWKINS Science and reason are certainly impressive powers to be reckoned with but Love may also be something that has long since been unrecognized to the faint of heart. What many scientists have often recognized to be the power of attraction in individuals often goes unrecognized as the power of love. LOVE AND SEPARATION In order to understand love and the greater sense of wholeness that it helps us to achieve in our lives, it is important that we first contend with the idea of separation. Just like the concept of attraction, the concept of separation is also a much wider concept that can be applied to almost every aspect of our universe. People become separated in their marriages but the concept of separation extends even further than just human relationships. Separation is something that science teaches us when we are just in grade school. We learn that objects can be divided into two halves. "The universe is incredibly large," says the teacher "and we are incredibly small." In the beginning, science teaches us about a universe of great complexity and we learn about this with eager eyes. We first learn that science is based on the necessary and useful idea of separation and yet, this very idea becomes something that is often a problem later in life. In order to cook our food, for instance, we need to know the scientific reason why the pots are separate from the pans. In order to serve the food, we need to know that the kitchen is separate from the dining room. Finally, in order to eat the meal, we need to know that the tables are separate from the chairs. This kind of knowledge is necessary for us to function and yet, it is not the kind of knowledge that really gives our lives meaning. It is not what gives our lives a lasting significance. Learning, itself, like the classrooms in which it occurs, is temporary. The ability to learn has no value when change is no longer necessary. The eternally creative have nothing to learn.10 – A COURSE IN MIRACLES Love is the thing that is found at the end of the road when all of our intricate concepts of separation and division will eventually leave us unfulfilled. Love rescues us from that split second with a completely different kind of perception. It comes to us directly and can even come in a single instant. In love, we have a larger vision of our dinner. We don't focus on the differences between the pots and the pans. We don't see just the tables and the chairs. Instead we have the impression of the entire house and our lovely mother as she makes us a delicious meal. In love, we eat the meal and feel grateful for all the things we have. We appreciate our family and the entire world around us. Love can turn the cottage into a golden palace.11 – GERMAN PROVERB

Love seeks to unify rather than divide. It seeks to experience rather than observe. Love is a tendency toward a larger vision and does not focus so heavily on the ideas of division and separation. Instead, these ideas are subordinate to it and they merely serve as tools for love's larger purpose. This surprising conclusion was in fact obtained through a nationwide inquiry of some of America's most eminent mathematicians. The study was intended to discover the mathematician's working methods for discovering new truths and new formulas. One of these mathematicians included Albert Einstein and the conclusion that was made was the following: Thinking plays only a subordinate part in the brief, decisive phase of the creative act itself.12 The missing link, which may help to explain many of the mysteries of science and eventually transform our entire way of looking at the world, may be love itself. It is only very recently that this connection between science and intuition is being understood in its wider significance. Science has become extremely useful in its manner of dividing and separating objects into parts. It has produced many new materials that can be used for hundreds of billions of tasks and ideas. The pinnacle of modern science has even lead to the grand discoveries of quantum theory and non-linear dynamics. These systems go so far as to incorporate the scientists themselves into the picture of what is going on. They begin to unify the scientist with the science. They open up a whole new world beyond the initial division and separation that first seemed so fundamental. The power of love goes even further to envision the workings of the universe as a unified whole. This power may teach us that nobody's truth is any better than another's. It can even go so far as to present a vision of unconditional love which sees all things as equally important in the totality of the universe. This underlying vision of equality is one of the main principles that eventually turn the power of attraction into the power of love. The secret of attraction is to love yourself. Attractive people judge neither themselves nor others. They are open to gestures of love. They think about love, and express their love in every action. They know that love is not a mere sentiment, but the ultimate truth at the heart of the universe.13 – DEEPAK CHOPRA Having come to a better understanding of the links between the power of attraction and the power of love, we can now go on to look at how attraction itself can grow to an even greater level of awareness into the awareness of love. The law of attraction can bring people to experience a larger vision than they had ever imagined and this is done through the power of our own thoughts. "We become what we think about" can be applied to larger and larger visions of the universe such that we can expand our own consciousness to greater and greater perspectives. The manner in which we do this is through an intimate understanding of the law of attraction .

understanding of the law of attraction .

Contents

The spiritual law of attraction stated in another way says that, "Whatever we hold in mind tends to manifest in our lives." This is an interpretation given to us from Dr. David R. Hawkins in many of his lectures and speeches around the world. It has also been expressed by Napoleon Hill. In general, it simply means that we tend to attract the things that we think about or focus on in our lives. By instilling our emotional energy into certain things, we call them toward us each day. Our minds become magnetized with the dominating thoughts we hold in our minds and these magnets attract to us the forces, the people, the circumstances of life which harmonize with the nature of our dominating thoughts.14 – NAPOLEON HILL Keeping a positive attitude certainly isn't an easy thing to do. Each day, people will tell themselves many negative things. These negative ideas will sometimes be expressed in the light of day by a seemingly happy person and yet, when we get to know the people who are thinking these ideas, we may find that they are actually quite depressed and afraid of many things. People make a lot of decisions based on these negative feelings and it isn't always apparent how much it is affecting their lives. It will often appear to be quite bad when you take a closer look inside. The negative tendencies that people pursue in their lives often help to confirm the initial fears that they have. They lose their jobs, their friends and their closest loved ones to problems that seem beyond their control. This seems impossible to change and yet, the law of attraction tells us something different. People's thoughts and decisions often promote the very kind of negative evidence that they initially set out to prove. They are the very cause of their own problems! The negative ideas that people project often function in a similar manner as a "self-fulfilling prophecy". By focusing on the negative, the negative comes to pass. The law of attraction tells us that, whatever we give our attention to becomes our point of attraction. It becomes the thing that we magnetize into our lives. This is even true for the things we try to separate ourselves from or fight against because we find that we are still giving these "negative" things our constant attention. Let's look at an example. Someone decides that the worst thing in the world would be for their loved one to leave them. They worry about this day and night. It is their worst fear and they can't get it out of their mind. As they focus on this fear, they find that they simply cannot trust the person they are with. They are constantly second guessing this person and accusing them of the fears they hold inside. Instead of showing them love and affection, they are actually driving this person away. When we create something, we always create it first in a thought form. If we are basically positive in attitude, expecting and envisioning pleasure, satisfaction and happiness, we will attract and create people, situations, and events which conform to our positive expectations.15 – SHAKTI GAWAIN Getting over our fears and negative emotions can be quite a challenge when we are applying the law of attraction in our lives. In order to be successful and attract what is positive, it is helpful to see the challenges ahead. If we know what to expect in terms of the law of attraction, we will be prepared to attract only the things that are truly best for us in our lives. In this way, we will avoid the fears and confusions and find the love and understanding along the way. OPPOSITES SEEM TO ATTRACT You've heard this said a million times and it certainly seems to be true in many cases. Opposites seem to attract. Oftentimes, couples seem as though they were two very different people. One is active, one is passive. One is cool and one is hot. Although these differences seem to exist on the surface, couples that stay together also have something more and this underlying vibration is the real thing that makes the attraction so powerful. People seem to be attracted to the qualities in another person that make them different. This is the way it appears on the surface and yet, this isn't the truth. As time goes on, the differences that seemed to attract these people no longer have the initial appeal that they first had. Couples who are mainly focused on the differences that we have with each other, tend to argue and even despise those same qualities that seemed so great in the beginning. They often find that they have nothing in common after they have been together for a little while. In this case, they may start to realize that they need some similarities in order to balance things out. Yin and yang tend to attract each other to create a balance but it is the underlying "balance" or "wholeness" that is really so attractive to these individuals. It is not the qualities of yin or yang themselves. An underlying vibration is necessary in order to keep those opposites together. The essential quality that is necessary to keep people together is often thought to be this wider vision of 'love' or 'peace'. Without this underlying power, the universe and the relationship would fly apart just like both Newton and Einstein might have helped us predict. Although it may be true that opposites seem to attract, it is an even greater truth that opposites are only kept together by an underlying vibration of love. This power of love is an even greater power of attraction that supersedes the powers of yin and yang and becomes, for many people, the supreme power of attraction in the universe. THE VOID Another challenging idea along the path to creating our own destiny involves the idea of the void. This is an idea which originates in the idea of separation and can be seen as a way of looking at life or at the universe. In simple terms, the void can best be understood in terms of the things that we WANT and the things that we DON'T WANT. If there is a thing that we DON'T WANT, we focus on it wherever we go and divide up our experiences in relation to this hidden idea of emptiness or "negation". The "void" is an idea that has been presented to many spiritual seekers along their path and this is actually a form of negative thinking that is very subtle and insidious to the advanced seeker. We all give power to our hidden negativities and they take on a larger and larger context as we develop. This context, when it reaches its widest conception, is something that eventually manifests as the "void". If we can look more closely at this idea and try to uncover the negativity in our own thinking, it may help us to open it into a wider context of awareness. This wider context would, by its very nature, be a more attractive context simply because of the larger awareness that it allows. First, let's look at an example. Some people are always dreading the future. They imagine that they will eventually have problems with their health or with their finances. They are always worried about what will happen to them down the road. After worrying about these outcomes, they find that they are very tired and need to take a break from the draining problems in their life. They decide to take a break from work because they are beginning to feel sick. They may stay home or even decide to quit their jobs because they "just can't take it anymore". "I hate my job" is one of the most common ideas that people tell themselves. "My relationships never work" is another common negation. With this kind of thinking, the future always seems to arrive with extreme predictability. Inevitably, negative people tend to be viewed by others as lazy or irresponsible. People don't want a negative person working at their company or hanging around their circle of friends. These people often lose their jobs and find themselves incapable of paying their bills after their relationships go sour. They are often abandoned by their mates and can even enter into a severe form of depression. Oftentimes, they will even develop health problems and find that all of their original predictions about the doom and gloom of the world have come true. Whoso diggeth a pit shall fall therein.16 – PROVERBS People who see a negative future become discontented. This seems obvious and yet, negative people seem intensely committed to their own negativity. It is as though they felt there was some great honor in seeing the bad side of things. The evidence they were looking for about the world and the negative "reality" of life always seems to arrive with predictable accuracy because the law of attraction is working in all areas of the universe. In order to stop this negative thinking, it is best to look at the way it manifests itself so as to uncover a larger field of attraction and open ourselves to more positive energies. RUNNING FROM FEAR If we decide to focus on fear and grief, we will surely attract these kinds of things into our life and feel a certain perverted satisfaction that our vision of negativity was initially correct. Even when we run from these fears, we cannot escape them. Running from fear only instills the energy into our lives and helps it to manifest as a reality. Running from fear is not the way to alleviate this negative emotion. In fact, battling with any kind of negative emotion is only another way of attracting it into our lives. If you have ever seen a person who is suffering from a mental illness, they can often be seen muttering to themselves or carrying on in a very strange manner. They may have acquired a sickness that paralyzes them in their lives. They will engage others with senseless arguments in order to satisfy their own sense of frustration or grief. What is so interesting is that others, who are less disturbed, will sometimes engage these people in elaborate discussions possibly in the hope of curing them or changing their minds. Quite often, the efforts are fruitless and only make the sane person appear worse off than when they began. When a sick person and a well person get together, it is more likely that the two will both end up sick rather than the two of them both becoming well. Engaging in a battle over negative ideas is likely to only produce more negative ideas so that nothing is solved. This same idea holds true when it comes to fear. Engaging our fear as though it were something we should be afraid of is not the correct course. Instead of running from the things we fear or fighting against the things we dislike, we might choose instead not to waste our energy. We might take the high road instead and choose not to give in to the secret attraction that these arguments may have. We might turn the other cheek and look for something more positive to pursue. Running from fear is only a way of expressing our own belief in the very power of fear. FDR's famous quote "We have nothing to fear but fear itself" profoundly suggests that fear is an empty idea with no power in and of itself. As long as we don't feed these fears, they will have nothing to live on and will eventually dissolve in the light of our own awareness. The law of attraction teaches us that this kind of positive thinking will only build on itself as we apply it in our lives. We begin to find that our courage is growing at enormous rates each day and the things we thought we should fear were only figments of our own imagination.

ACCEPTING OUR GRIEF Depression is a similar energy as fear but it is also a very common and natural phase of a person's development. As we learn to incorporate the negative ideas that we encounter in life, we also learn to reach for a larger context in which to understand these negative emotions. This larger context may eventually lead to a healthier attitude but this certainly doesn't happen overnight. As we begin to identify our negative emotions, fear and grief will begin to dissolve. The outside will eventually conform to our inner vision of things as we put the law of attraction into action. It takes a lot of practice to overcome sadness and grief in our everyday lives and sometimes these emotions can go on for years. Oftentimes, people will turn to anti-depressant medication as a way of helping them get over these negative emotions. Anti-depressants can be very helpful in learning how to turn away from negative ideas and emotions and to incorporate more positive habits into our lives. Experiencing grief or depression can be seen as a positive step toward spiritual growth even if we need to turn to some help from science and medicine. We eventually discover that we were the inventors of those fears and that there wasn't any realistic basis for them in the first place. Looking at our own depression and sadness is a necessary phase of development and can be viewed in a positive light if we allow ourselves the chance to grow. The true reality in the universe is love but coming to this awareness is often a very long and arduous process. Eventually, we find the strength to view our grief as a temporary illusion that can also be dissolved in the light of consciousness.

The opposite of love is fear, but what is all-encompassing can have no opposite.17 – A COURSE IN MIRACLES Many of our negative impressions come from an underlying belief that everything is useless, empty and essentially a large void. People often talk about a sense of emptiness in their lives and a void in their hearts that simply cannot be filled no matter what they do. If this void were truly the ultimate reality of the universe, then there would certainly be a good reason to assume that everything was ultimately negative. This, however, is simply not the case as both science and spirituality have come to show us. The one simple understanding that someone can have about "nothingness" is that, by its own very definition it is "Not". POSITIVE REFLECTIONS ON THE VOID According to the great masters and many of the more modern interpretations of science, anything that can be perceived or thought of is always considered to be subjective in some sense. This is why the law of attraction works so well in our lives. Ideas about "nothingness" or the "void" do not have any real existence apart from a person's subjective experience. We are the ultimate creators of our own reality and coming to this realization is the only thing we need to do before our own happiness can become a priority. We eventually learn that there could never be a "void" if there were not someone like us to experience it in the first place. The observer, our Self, is the subjective reality which becomes the very proof that the "void" does not exist. We become our own proof about the reality of the world around us. This has been the natural progression of many great mystics over time, many of whom have experienced deep periods of depression or what is often called 'The Dark Night of the Soul' before they have reached Enlightenment. Eckhart Tolle has expressed this idea about his own fear and the idea of the "void" in his book The Power of Now. I could feel myself being sucked into a void. It felt as though the void was inside myself rather than outside. Suddenly, there was no more fear, and I let myself fall into that void. I have no recollection of what happened after that. I was awakened by the chirping of a bird outside the window. I had never heard such a sound before.....Tears came into my eyes.....I recognized the room, and yet I knew that I had never truly seen it before...For the next five months, I lived in a state of uninterrupted deep peace and bliss.18 Eckhart Tolle's experience of the "void" was an extremely profound experience and one that he seemed to attract into his life before he found the ability to overcome it and thereby let it go. After his experience, it is plain to see that another focus took over his attention and the negative ideas were seen as truly non-existent. Tolle could not recollect anything from his experience of the void because such an experience is actually non-existent in ultimate reality. He went on to have many subsequent experiences which had a positive quality because he let go of his false conception of the void. Theodore Nottingham has also expressed a similar idea about negative emotions in his reference to the teachings of Peter Ouspensky.

The purpose of dealing with negative emotions is to a) clean up our inner life so that b) we can use the energies precisely for experiences of higher consciousness.19 – PETER OUSPENSKY After working on our negative emotions for so long, a saturation point is eventually reached and a new realization crystallizes in our minds. In terms of the grand lesson that many spiritual teachers have tried to impart to us, Dr. David R. Hawkins' published works are widely recognized as evidence of a very advanced state of spiritual awareness such as the one being discussed here. Dr. Hawkins has also spoken extensively on the idea of the "void" and has given valuable insights into the interpretation of this idea about "nothingness" in spiritual experience. Void is a state created solely by the mind's belief in it as an actual possibility. The only actual possibilities in Reality are Is-ness, Allness and Beingness. It is obvious that theoretical opposites to these would then be conceived.20 – HAWKINS Although theoretical opposites to what "Is" are often conceived, these opposites are only temporary diversions from the truth. They are not accurate pictures of reality. Dr. Hawkins explains that concepts such as "off" when used to designate the condition of a light switch, do not actually refer to a separate state. "Off" is merely a convenient idea that we use to designate what would more accurately be referred to as "not on".Although this sounds like an insignificant point, Dr. Hawkins explains that it is actually very significant to our underlying perceptions about the world around us. We keep imagining that there are objective realities to the negative ideas we possess. Dr. Hawkins stresses the importance of understanding that there is never an actual state of "offness" in an electrical circuit but only the presence of electricity or the absence of electricity. 21 The problems that we experience between love and separation always stem from a misconception that there are certain states in our lives where there is "lack" or "emptiness". Lack or emptiness, however, is simply not a reality that holds any true existence beyond our own perception of it. Without realizing what we are doing, we attract certain ideas into our lives. Oftentimes we cannot see this because we don't see the immense power that our minds possess. We find later that we are very depressed and experiencing a sense of emptiness in our lives but we don't know why. Many spiritual practices attempt to get us to a place where we are feeling good more of the time. If we can eliminate our negative tendencies, then we tend to attract more positive things that improve our feelings. Ideas, in general, tend to be magnetic. They attract more of the same and we see a momentum that eventually starts to go in the right direction. By gently guiding our thoughts and our feelings to a better place, we become more adept at this practice. We learn to take a nice walk when we are feeling bad or spend some time in appreciation of nature. We learn meditation and how to guide our thoughts and emotions into a more harmonious stream and the good events will only follow once we learn to change our minds. In a universe that is based upon the law of attraction, what could be more important than our own good feelings? ATTRACTOR FIELDS Although love is considered to be a power even greater than reason, science itself has certainly come a long way in explaining the power of attraction. Modern medicine can do wondrous things to help us along to a better vision of reality and help to boost us out of the negative thinking that we originally had entrained ourselves into. The tendency of more and more people to reach a more holistic vision of reality is getting closer and closer everyday. The progress of science has continued in recent decades with the advancement of non-linear dynamics and, what is known as, "Chaos theory" in science. Despite its inherent challenges, science has continued to press on and to champion more and more elaborate explanations about the power of attraction. In recent years, the new science of nonlinear dynamics has posed the idea of 'strange attractors' which help to explain more about our objects' behavior in the universe. 'Attractor field' is a term derived from nonlinear dynamics and signifies that within what appears to be random or unconnected occurrences, there is actually an invisible, organizing pattern field of influence that affects the occurrence of phenomena within each level of consciousness.22 – HAWKINS Scientists now believe that the universe may be just a large conglomeration of attractor patterns under which all of nature is guided. These attractor patterns might be viewed as the underlying cause or 'Mind' of the universe with which science is learning more and more everyday. In this sense, the decision making process may be part of a much larger and more essential pattern of attraction that we are only just beginning to understand in our modern conception of scientific understanding. The decision making process is a function of consciousness itself; the mind makes choices based on millions of pieces of data and their correlations and projections, far beyond conscious comprehension, and with enormous rapidity. This is a global function dominated by energy patterns that the new science of nonlinear dynamics terms 'attractors'.23 – HAWKINS Dr. David R. Hawkins is a leading scientist and lecturer on the topic of both science and spirituality. He has introduced the idea that the underlying cause of people's behavior, and of the activities in nature, are actually guided by these larger 'attractor fields' which are thought of as 'fields of consciousness'. These different fields organize the behavior of objects in nature and tend to attract things into their field according to a greater degree of order that they inspire. Although he is not an advocate of any particular field in general, one of the larger attractor fields that Dr. Hawkins has spoken of is the field of Taoism or "The Tao". TAOISM

Taoism is a great spiritual tradition which is based on the teachings of Lao-tzu. The Tao, in the broadest sense, is the way the universe functions, the path taken by natural events. It is characterized by spontaneous creativity and by the regular changes of phenomena. Through the techniques and practices of Taoism, many dedicated followers have claimed to achieve a greater harmony in their lives and a wider expansion of consciousness. For them, the incoherent has become coherent and they have finally experienced a grand vision of peace and order in their lives. To the mind that is still, the whole universe surrenders.24 – LAO-TZU Taoism teaches that, in nature, spring follows from winter and day follows from night. These cycles, that we also learn about in our science classes, proceed without effort. The Tao has always been considered to be the way of the universe; the norm, the rhythm, and the guiding power behind nature. It is important to recognize, however, that the Tao is spirit, not matter. It is an inexhaustible energy that flows stronger the more it is drawn upon. It is an energy which is very similar to the energy of Love. Love focuses on giving to others and transforming rather than controlling. If the power underlying all of nature were similar to the Power of Love, then Lao-Tzu would have been right even long before the scientists had begun theorizing about the workings of the stars. The reason why the universe is eternal is that it does not live for itself; it gives life to others as it transforms.25 – LAO-TZU The goal of Taoists is to attain harmony with the Tao. This attainment of harmony with the Tao is also seen as living in accord with nature. Nature is something that should not be exploited and abused, it should be befriended and appreciated. The ideal man in Taoism is one who, through the naturalness of his existence, becomes self-sufficient and not dependent upon wealth or social realms. In this way, true happiness can be found. The yin-yang doctrine is based on the concept that there are continuous transformations within the Tao. The principle that embraces nature is divided into two opposites or principles that oppose one another. The principles of yang are light, heat, Heaven, male and sun. The principles of the yin are darkness, cool, earth, female and moon. Everything consists of this balance. The production of yin from yang and yang from yin occurs in a cyclical motion. It is continuous and it happens in such as way so that no principle ever dominates the other. Yin and Yang express the contrasting aspects and interrelationships of everything in the universe. For a Taoist, the objective is to reach and maintain harmony with the Tao. When this harmony is reached enlightenment has been achieved. In Enlightenment, we accept the plainness of our life. The truths of the Tao cannot be found in any doctrine. Instead, they are found when a person's energy is balanced and their mind is clear. Taoism promotes simplicity, openness, and wisdom. Once you have realized it, you have openness to life, a tranquility of mind and a reserved genius. The Taoist sage is not arrogant and does not discriminate between opposites. They are indifferent to worldly affairs and are at peace. In such loving attraction live earth and sky: As when blessed rain falls soft upon the earth, Mankind and Part II. The Law of Attraction www.guideforliving.com 29 Nature could unite like lovers — Free of law, free of command, People would finally be at peace.26 – LAO-TZU As we develop our understanding of the Tao, we learn to incorporate its ideas into our own lives and to experience a more profound sense of harmony all around us. Things start to work much better in our lives and there seems to be a lot less problems to contend with. The power of both attraction and love are working in our life to bring us to a greater sense of wholeness and unity each day. Although we are constantly attracted by the experiences that these higher fields of consciousness can bring, we also find that our old habits tend to return to us and are always pulling us back down into the more narrow energy fields that we initially experienced in our lives. These lower fields of energy still exist in other people and other places. We only learn to change our lifestyles by aligning ourselves with the wider attractor fields of both love and peace. COMMITMENT Choosing a direction is the first step in aligning ourselves with wider attractor fields. Commitment is the element of attraction that makes the journey a likely success because things start to take on a quality of permanence. This is obvious in human relationships but not as commonly understood in terms of spiritual pursuits. Commitment can keep a marriage together but can also make a spiritual journey a grand success. Until one is committed there is hesitating, the chance to draw back, always ineffectiveness. Concerning all acts of initiative (and creation), there is one elementary truth, the ignorance of which kills countless ideas and splendid plans. That the moment one definitely commits oneself, Providence moves, too. All sorts of things occur to help one that would never otherwise have occurred. A whole stream of events issues from the decision, raising in one's favor all manner of unforeseen incidents and meetings and material assistance which no man could have dreamed would have come his way. – JOHAN WOLFGANG VON GOETHE Goethe knew that nothing can come about until there is commitment. This is true because the law of attraction will only allow us to have the things we think about each day. Until we are committed to placing our energy in one certain area, the success of our endeavors cannot be realized. Goethe also expressed this sentiment in relation to the power of love when he said, "We are shaped and fashioned by what we love." It would seem from his ideas that we are not only affected by the things we focus on in our minds, but especially by the things we love.

focus on in our minds, but especially by the things we love.

1

Career

Once we begin to recognize that our old way of seeing things is attracting negative things into our lives, we begin to feel the attraction to become something else. We begin to focus on the things we love and this takes place in greater and greater intensity as we adopt a wider view of the world around us. We learn to accept things and to even experience gratitude for the way things are because this brings more joy and happiness to us. It is a difficult task at first as our old ways of seeing the world tend to permeate every area of our lives and negativity has become a very bad habit. It is even hard, in the beginning, to root out our negative emotions as their source tends to be very cunning and hidden from our view. In our work and at home we can especially see that we have established many bad habits that keep us stuck in the more narrow fields of consciousness and the magnetic power of these old ways is very hard to overcome. The difficulty of inner work results from the great effort required to escape from the familiar gravity of lower attractor fields and move to the influence of a higher field.– HAWKINS In order to arrive at this higher level of consciousness, we eventually find that we must begin to apply a new awareness to every aspect of our lives. The spiritual effort becomes a daily practice that we apply to our careers and our relationships. At first the efforts seem very difficult but eventually we come to see that something else has been working in our lives which is far beyond our own personal power and has begun helping us along the way. In fact, this power has been there all along but we were not aware of its presence until now. Our careers require extreme amounts of time and effort in our lives and yet, this area is often relegated to the 'back burner' when we think about spirituality. We think of our spiritual lives as a time to read or meditate and our careers as a time to make money and survive. Nothing could be further from the truth. Our careers are an intricate element of our spiritual lives and an area that needs considerable attention if we are going to attract positive energy into our lives. We will have to learn to think more positively about our careers if we are going to attract positive energy throughout our entire day. A career involves more than just a job. A career involves a progression or an increase that brings us toward a greater level of success in our job. This happens by becoming more advanced in our spiritual pursuits. It is often a surprise to many people who practice spirituality that some of the most successful career minded individuals are also some of the most spiritual people in the world. It is the underlying drive to succeed that fuels people's desire to have a career and facing the daily challenges of a career is a great way to improve ourselves. DESTRUCTIVE THINKING Many people are dead set against money and careers. A common sentiment is that "money is the root of all evil" and many Americans believe that the corporations and the government are only out to exploit people for power and control. Money is often set in a bad light by those of us who may study spirituality or religion. The Eastern traditions often emphasize the importance of being "unattached" to wealth and success so that many people misunderstand the intentions of corporations or millionaires who are in possession of great wealth. Having a lot of money does not necessarily mean that there is going to be an attachment to money. Indeed, the Biblical quote alluded to above actually reads "The love of money is the root of all evil."29 (1 Timothy 6: 10, my emphasis) Many great millionaires become philanthropists and help to solve enormous problems all over the world. It is the attitude that we carry toward wealth and power that creates the attachment that many religions often speak of. This is an idea which is very often misunderstood and which often leads to destructive thinking. This misconception about the meaning of "attachment" often leads many people to think that you have to be poor and unemployed in order to be spiritual. A reverse sort of egotism can even set up with this kind of thinking where people will oftentimes see themselves to be 'better' than the rich and successful simply because they don't have any money or success themselves. As time goes on, these less fortunate people become unhappy in their lives because the rewards they imagined themselves to eventually gain for their commitment to poverty were somehow not materializing in the way they had hoped. They become angry at the world as if some mysterious enemy had taken over their lives and made them fall into a terrible misfortune. This problem only comes about as a result of people's negative thinking. They imagine a future when everything will fall apart for the rich and successful and they will get their just rewards. The future never arrives for having lived a life of poverty and unemployment and they wonder "What went wrong?" The attachments of the ego take place in all areas of the world and not just for the rich and successful minded people. A career can certainly become a place where people abuse their powers and exploit the less fortunate people of the world but it is also a place where the less fortunate can become bitter and resentful. The world around them simply becomes dark and hopeless because they never made the effort to overcome their unfortunate state. They hate the people in power and resent the larger order that has come to exist around them. Overcoming this kind of negative thinking is extremely hard. We have to start to consider the possibility that powerful people may only be doing their best to make the world a better place. We may not understand who the corrupt people are and who the philanthropists are until we have walked a mile in their shoes. A better place to focus our energies would be in our own lives and on our own negative thinking. In this way, we may learn to overcome these destructive thoughts and lead ourselves out of the negative patterns we have set up in our lives. CONSTRUCTIVE THINKING A career is the perfect place to set up your spiritual workshop because it is an area that requires a great deal of time and energy everyday and involves almost every aspect of spiritual principles in order that you make it successful. Even if you are starting out at the very bottom as a dishwasher in a hot and dirty kitchen, you can make your career into an intensely spiritual pursuit that will eventually lead to other jobs and a more productive career that brings happiness and joy. Everyone needs a job of some kind in order to feel productive and the simplest or the most complex jobs are equally fertile ground for spiritual practices. The key to long term success is not in the particular job that you are doing. The key is in working on yourself as you do your particular job. This is constructive thinking because it makes it possible to use your time even more productively. When there is not an extremely important task immediately at hand, you can focus your mind on the present moment and simply experience your own inner consciousness. This effort will eventually widen the attractor field in which you find yourself and open up greater amounts of energy into your life. If you make sure and work harder on yourself than you do on your particular job, success will surely follow wherever you go. Once you begin dedicating hours a day to your personal development, your success will not be far behind. THE DETAILS OF LIFE Oftentimes, spiritual enthusiasts may tend to think that it is 'ok' to avoid the details of life because spirituality is associated with keeping things 'simple'. We think we should live simple lives and we can ignore the details. We don't worry about mortgages or going to the dentist or sorting through the mail. We like to wear sandals and meditate. We like to feed the pigeons and sit on a park bench. Keeping life simple is certainly an essential spiritual principle but paying attention to the details of life is also something that we shouldn't be afraid of. Looking at the details doesn't have to mean looking at the details of 'worry' and 'fear'. The details can in fact be extremely beautiful. Here are a few details that we certainly don't have to worry about and that don't help us to move forward in our lives. First of all, we don't have to worry about the detail of "urgency". Urgency suggests that things aren't exactly as they need to be and therefore the universe has somehow been created 'wrong'. This is a negative idea that only feeds the flames of our discontent. We don't have to worry about the detail of "being in a hurry" because we now feel confident that everything is happening for a reason. Similarly, we don't have to worry about the detail of "recognition" or the detail of "popularity" when we go about making a career for ourselves. If we have faith in the larger attractor fields, we know that our just rewards will eventually come to us after we have taken care of the more important issues at hand. Finally, we don't have to worry about the detail of "tomorrow" and this idea is very eloquently expressed in the first book of the New Testament. Can any of you by worrying add a single hour to the span of your life? ... So do not worry about tomorrow, for tomorrow will bring worries of its own. Today's trouble is enough for today.30 –MATT. 6:27, 34 Details that consume us never help to accomplish anything worthwhile in the end and it is easy to overlook the important details when we are running around like a chicken with our heads cut off. We may simply be trying too hard to control the wrong things and so the more important details tend to elude us. Eventually we have no energy left for the most important things which are the experience of joy and happiness in our lives.

experience of joy and happiness in our lives.

Once we've learned to look for spiritual truth, we will begin to find it in every area of our lives. This will especially be true in terms of the details. The details of a beautiful flower will be seen in the same way as the details of the pile of mail at the front door. Even a can of garbage can be seen as beautiful, as Dr. Hawkins notably states: One adds the pathway of the heart by making a decision to be unconditionally loving to all that is encountered..... This means one has to learn to love even a garbage can. When seen correctly, garbage cans are not only loveable but beautiful and perfect...... When the beauty and loveableness of the beat-up old garbage can reveals itself, the spiritual seeker can affirm that they are well along the way.31 – HAWKINS After we have calmed down and begun to attract more positive energies into our lives, all the details of life become stunningly beautiful and full of promise. We can return to the details about the mortgage and the dentist which at first seemed so fraught with worry and fear. We may begin to see great opportunities in the pile of mail instead of endless problems and worries in each bill. The details of life provide us with a great opportunity to experience beauty and joy but only if we approach them with the right attitude. If we carry an attitude of worry and fear, the details will also express this back to us as objects of worry and fear. If we carry an attitude of joy and gratitude, the details of life will express these more positive ideas instead. Little jobs can also be a joy if we learn to practice a spiritual presence in our lives. A wider success will eventually come from what first seemed like an unimportant detail in life and success will become the rule instead of the exception. Don't be afraid to give your best to what seemingly are small jobs. Every time you conquer one it makes you that much stronger. If you do the little jobs well, the big ones tend to take care of themselves.32 – DALE CARNEGIE Letting the big jobs take care of themselves is a profound idea but something that should not be misunderstood in terms of being 'lazy' or apathetic. We don't ignore the importance of the big jobs when we take on the attention to the smaller ones. It simply becomes the case that we understand we aren't in control of the big jobs. We control only the little things and keep the big jobs at the forefront of our awareness. By staying aware of what is ultimately most important, we actually call this into our lives according to the law of attraction. One of the greatest examples of this kind of behavior can be seen in the activity of thousands of individual ants. Each of them has one small job to do but they also have a larger pattern in mind as they work together to create an elaborate ant colony. Underneath the seemingly small attention to detail that each ant displays, is the larger vision of the colony. The queen ant is often seen as the 'leader' and yet she never gives any direct orders to the ants. The queen doesn't "tell" the ants what to do. Each ant reacts to its own individual scent and leaves its own chemical trail which provides a stimulus to the other ants. This is the law of attraction working in each ant's life. Genetics and other factors certainly play a role in the "decisions" of each ant but there is still an autonomous presence in each ant so that they can make their own decisions within the larger framework. Despite the lack of a central "leader", ant colonies still have an amazingly complex pattern of behavior and individual ants have even been shown to be capable of solving complex geometric problems. An example of this is the fact that ants commonly determine the furthest distance from each of the entrances to their hills in order to know where the best place to dispose of their dead. The ants individually measure the distance between hills in order to locate the grave sites for other ants. This is a higher order of consciousness at work and something that reflects the greater good of each member of the colony.

This larger vision of order and harmony that can be seen in the behavior of ants and many other groups of animals, is a necessary element behind the energy which contributes to the completion of even the smallest jobs in our world. The larger spiritual energy fields are acted on through the individual attention to the smaller details in life. These more detailed jobs become the active purpose of our daily experience through their connection to the larger purpose. The larger vision fuels the smaller attention to detail and each of us can then move along to a greater and greater awareness of what is. EMERGENCE IN CAREER In science, the concept of 'emergence' can be used to describe the way small jobs are ultimately related to their larger attractor fields. This concept of emergence helps to explain how these smaller, simpler tasks receive a spiritual energy through their connection to the larger whole. This is the idea that more complex patterns arise from the more simple details of our behavior. For an activity to be thought of as 'emergent' it is generally seen as unpredictable from a lower level. To the casual observer, it may appear as though the person is simply doing a very menial task that is unimportant. It is unpredictable and unprecedented, however, when the reasons for this simple behavior beome more apparent in terms of a larger scheme. Although they cannot be explained by reference to typical explanations, a more complex explanation helps them to make sense.33 In a typical job, a common reason for taking that job may be 'money' or 'opportunity for promotion'. These are common ideas that serve as simple reasons for going to work. They are fairly simplistic but are still commonly held to be the driving force behind many people's careers. If a person is doing the job in order to increase their spiritual connection, however, this may represent a new level in the system's evolution. This would be an example of an emergent pattern that could not be readily observable from simply looking at the individual person. It is a pattern that gives a greater significance to the person's job and would ultimately become more apparent as time went on because the persons career would begin to visibly reflect this hidden dimension. As the person's career progressed, the emergent pattern would be an extremely helpful and productive pattern of activity that could be seen more as a property of the collective whole rather than just a simple financial pattern. In many cases, a person's behavior in their job cannot be explained according to lower level reasoning. Many physical properties in nature are the same such as that of molecules which transmit sound. There aren't any specific qualities in the molecules which explain the larger pattern of behavior such as the transmission of sound. Emergent structures are patterns seen from a single event or a simple rule and yet they are still inherent in each individual part of the system.

Although there is nothing that is immediately evident as an explanation for the behavior, the interactions of each part in relation to the larger whole lead to an order and harmony that can be seen by each person.

MONEY

Money is one of the most common explanations that people use to describe the reasoning behind their job. It is an extremely simple explanation and yet it is often considered less than adequate to bring complete happiness in their lives. "I've got to pay the bills" is a simple yet insufficient reason for obtaining joy and harmony in our work. If we are to experience real happiness and a strong purpose in our jobs, we must typically involve ourselves more intimately with our job performance and make some kind of alternate contribution either to the larger purpose of the company or to ourselves. Money plays an important part in this sense but other factors such as improving our quality of life also plays a role. Successful people make money. It's not that people who make money become successful, but that successful people attract money. They bring success to what they do.[34] – WAYNE DYER

Donald Trump has expressed the importance of money in terms of "a scorecard that tells me I've won and by how much". Trump is one of the most successful real estate developers of the modern age. He is more associated with wealth and money than even Bill Gates, who is the richest man in the world. Donald Trump has explained that his happiness really doesn't come from the money but from the business dealings themselves. Trump obtains his joy in 'making the deal' and this only happens to generate large amounts of money as a byproduct. He certainly pays attention to the money but the real joy is located in the 'deal'. If Donald Trump couldn't make deals, he simply wouldn't be happy.[35] The pattern that emerges in the career of Donald Trump is one of many successful 'deal makers'. At first glance, people see the money as the motivating factor because it is the simplest and most easy explanation. Of course, the money scorecard is definitely important but it isn't the whole picture. When we look closer, we see a more complex pattern emerging. In other fields, money may also have a certain ability to serve as a scorecard but this scorecard may become less useful as we move into more subjective fields of work. Art, for example, is not always judged so well through its monetary value and yet, it can still be a very good way to make some initial judgments. In terms of money and our careers, we will always have to take into consideration the importance of this simple explanation but this is only an initial way of seeing the larger pattern in a career. As we begin to focus our spiritual efforts in our job and career, a larger pattern may eventually emerge which can bring even greater success.

GOAL SETTING

One of the most important elements to having a successful career is to think big. The more you are able to put into your mind, the better things you are going to achieve. Earl Nightengale has also said that a person's common problem is not that they can't achieve their goal, but that they never set the proper goals that they need to be successful. Setting the right goals is a very big part of achievement itself. A goal is sort of like having a dream that includes a specific deadline. The more detailed the goal is, the better. "Having a million dollars" is a great goal but it isn't a very detailed one. A goal needs to explain the useful aspects that are going to assist you in your achievement.36 Daily habits are a great way to fill out the details of a realistic goal. We have to make sure our work ethic will match with our dreams and ask ourselves if we are dedicated enough to carry through with the effort. The financial rewards are only one small part of a realistic goal. They will not typically work as a sole motivator in our career. Attention to spiritual values in our careers can bring about a more comprehensive practice which can then return to us as a worthy investment in the future. We will eventually learn to function in a productive way with the other people in our lives who will help to make us more successful as we move along our career path.

2

Relationships

Relationships are often what inspire us each morning to get out of bed and make an effort to improve our lives. The power of attraction is never more obvious than in the case of two people in love. This power makes each of us more eager and willing to make that extra effort in our lives and to go on with each successive day. The power in a relationship is also the thing which fuels people's sense of spiritual effort in their lives and gives them a sense of gratitude for their life. ROMANCE Romance is one of the most powerful energies that inspire an interest in the spiritual life. It is the romantic ideal that is so intimately tied to our experience of love and ultimately to the greater meaning behind life. – how fortunate are you and I, whose home is timelessness: we who have wandered down from fragrant mountains of eternal now to frolic in such mysteries as birth and death a day(or maybe even less)27 – E.E. CUMMINGS Some of the most romantic ideas have been expressed to us through art and poetry and these fields are especially disposed to inspire a greater vision of what is sacred and most important to us in our lives. Romance is also closely associated with love as it helps to express the challenges that are encountered when two people strive to have a loving relationship. Love is always fraught with challenges and romance helps us to express these challenges in a more positive light.One of the more widely held beliefs about romantic love is that there is often a mere 'randomness' to the encounter which eventually can be seen to have a wider significance in the more meaningful pattern of love. Romantic love is also commonly thought to involve an overcoming of obstacles in which the larger pattern is somehow threatened by a less meaningful element. Romantic love cannot be controlled and is therefore thought to be something beyond the individuals themselves. The pattern of romantic love initially emerged in the Middle Ages when it was often the case that insurmountable barriers would separate two would-be lovers from their true destiny of eternal union. This is the typical image that we have when we think of romantic visions. The overcoming of age-old barriers often results in a strong regard for 'winning the love' of the other person and it has motivated great efforts to be expressed through poetry, songs and heroic battles since the earliest ages. Even today, writers go to great efforts to express this ongoing struggle and to revive the old passions of the earlier romantic ideal. We strive to express these ideas in the same way that we always have because the themes are always the same and will never change. We think, sometimes, there's not a dragon left. Not one brave night, not a single princess gliding Through secret forests, enchanting deer and Butterflies with her smile...... What a pleasure to be wrong. Princesses, knights, enchantments and dragons, mystery and adventure .....not only are they here-and-now, they're all that ever lived on earth! – RICHARD BACH

In our modern age, romantic love is still the theme of many forms of art and entertainment. Popular culture, as it is expresses through films and music is rich with romantic love. While romantic love is still the dream of many, some claim that the more modern presentations of the media are still not realistic. Romantic love, as depicted in books and movies, is thought to be extremely rare and may not ever occur at all. Critics point at the modern dating practices in which sex is really the only true goal of the partners and a lasting relationship is almost never the case. Many people also suggest that the rigorous demands of money and careers often rob people of the romantic ideal and that the wider vision of love can never be realized. MODERN DAY DRAGONS Modern statistics and the many observations of psychologists also paint a somewhat dim picture about romantic love. Although love is certainly thought to be a reality that is possible in our age, it is often represented in the mass media as something other than realistic. The dragons of the modern age may still be alive and well but their imaginary quality may now come to us in a completely different way. Many argue that the modern day dragons are intimately connected to the mass media in the way that it presents love as a romantic fantasy rather than a higher level of spiritual awareness. Love as depicted in the mass media is not what this level is about. What the world generally refers to as 'love' is an intense emotional condition, combining physical attraction, possessiveness,

control, addiction, eroticism and novelty. It's usually fragile and fluctuating, waxing and waning with varying conditions.39 – HAWKINS It may certainly be that love is still a realistic goal to obtain in our lives but many of the false ideas about romantic love may have to first be addressed if we are to overcome its obstacles in the modern age. We may need a new way of looking at romantic love that will help us to find our true destiny and a lasting relationship. Hidden underneath the temporary attractiveness of the common romantic notions will hopefully lie an attention to our own spiritual practices and a more serious concern for the law of attraction. GROWTH IN RELATIONSHIPS As the attraction to the higher levels of awareness intensifies in our lives, an underlying vibration will become the glue that holds a relationship together. Attraction becomes more than just a temporary relationship between two people but rather a balancing force that continues to make each partner attractive to the other. The individuals move out into the world and begin to establish relationships in their careers and social lives so that they learn to practice the principles of love with everyone they meet. This is a further advancement in awareness that could be understood as the tendency toward unconditional love. Love is often considered to be a power that can endure for eternity because it strives toward a unity between all things rather than just two people. This eternal nature is also a tendency toward unconditional love as it incorporates not only the two individuals who were first attracted to each other but others whom they meet after they have first fallen in love. Growing couples learn to share their love with the others around them and move forward toward a more eternal vision of love. The tendency toward unconditional love may begin when a couple decides to move forward as individuals, either in their careers or in the case of a family. FAMILY Starting a family has always been the natural progression that a couple in love will embark upon. Just like the challenges they first face in their romantic love, the challenges they face with children are often profoundly underestimated. A mother and father must endure many more responsibilities than they ever imagined and arguments over how to raise the children are often at the top of the list when it comes to disagreements between spouses. The law of attraction applies here just as it has applied in every circumstance before. We become what we think about as individuals and as a family. It is interesting to see the way children often take on very different roles from their parents. They have minds of their own and there really is no way of controlling them. In the same way that couples tend to create a balance between them, families also tend to move toward a balance and various roles will come into play so as to carry on this underlying vibration of wholeness and totality in the family. It is important to remember that we can only control the small things but not the big things. Family members will all have different visions of what is right for them and we must be open to the individual differences of each person. If the par ents are to continue to strive for the higher level of awareness that they reached in their own relationship, they will have to continue to apply this to their children who eventually introduce new challenges to the family dynamic. It seems as though the original idea that opposites attract would be showing its colors once again and yet a family will not stay together unless there is an underlying set of values which hold the entire unit together. Family patterns and family structure have changed alot in the past few decades. However, it is still a great advantage for children if they are encouraged to pursue positive and worthwhile values in their everyday lives. Some of the more basic core values that help to promote a positive attractiveness are the pursuit of personal development, independence and responsibility, leadership, citizenship, respect for others and a positive enjoyment of life. In the case of personal development, children should be encouraged to develop physically, emotionally and mentally. They should learn positive values that are related to their health, learning, creativity and exploration. These may include the ability to trust themselves and others through the use of open communication and genuine concern. Healthy competition that springs from a mutual support can also be emphasized. These attractive values help to contribute to the positive development of any individual and they are essential to promoting a better quality of life. In terms of independence, a child should be provided with an individual sense of freedom but should also learn personal responsibility and self-control. Activities that allow them to act independently and responsibly will encourage an attractiveness toward these values in greater proportions .

over time. Parents should allow children to make mistakes and then to learn from those mistakes. The children can learn to become involved in the planning and execution of their own future in a manner that promotes their own independence and personal responsibility. Leadership is also an important value to promote in the family as it is closely tied to independence and responsibility. Many experts believe that leadership qualities emerge naturally as long as parents promote the values of being positive and enjoying the many opportunities that life has to offer. Parents can reinforce these ideals, however, by modelling the more positive and constructive values in their own families. Citizenship is a higher level value that children can benefit from as it helps them to recognize the value of the democratic process and their own role as a citizen in a democracy. Parents should recognize that their opinions, ideas and values will strongly affect the perceptions of their children and eventually affect their overall attitude about their own careers and work ethic in the larger community. Learning to respect others is probably one of the most important values that children can benefit from as it teaches them how to become attractive and to ultimately love another person. Respect is intimately connected to responsibility. Our responsibility to each other is what makes our relationships both lasting and loving. Children can learn that it is their own responsibility to see their behavior as having an impact upon others in either a positive or negative way and this will teach them to develop better relationships. Finally, a positive enjoyment of life is probably the most central value that a child can learn. Life can be seen as great! It can have adventures, surprises and lots of joy. Eventually they may become leaders who inspire others by the way they perceive life. Problems can be seen as challenges to be overcome and as positive learning experiences rather than permanent obstacles. By incorporating the many values already mentioned and others such as courtesy, acceptance, compassion and integrity, a family will become an attractive field of spiritual values where the members can thrive and grow. The law of attraction can be implemented in a positive way for both individuals and families so as to bring about a healthy manner of living.

healthy manner of living.

3

Health

law of attraction to our physical bodies

Applying the law of attraction to our physical bodies is probably one of the most common applications that people use. We commonly think of attraction as something that has to do with personal appearance and we associate a healthy body with an attractive person. Maintaining our health will certainly make us more attractive and will also promote more positive thoughts and emotions. A healthy body leads to a healthy state of mind and maintaining these two things is all part of a positive spiritual approach. NUTRITION Nutrition is one of the most important elements of maintaining a strong body. A positive attitude toward nutrition will attract more information into your life about better and easier diets so that eventually your daily eating habits will become effortless. It is extremely important to have a good diet that will ensure the proper ratio of macro and micronutrients in the daily regimen. This nutritional concern will aid the body in its recovery process after a strenuous exercise and also maintain a general level of health and well being. Adhering to a low-intake diet takes a lot of the stress off the bodies internal functions and makes it a lot easier to maintain a healthy weight over time. This is just another example of the law of attraction taking effect in our lives. EXERCISE Physical exercise is also one of the most highly recommended ways of achieving a good overall health in the body. This can be focused in various athletic abilities or just a regular physical exercise. Whichever method we choose, it is The Law of Attraction proven that physical exercise is paramount in the prevention of many diseases such as cancer, diabetes, cardiovascular disease, and obesity. Exercises can be divided into three groups; flexibility exercises, aerobic exercises and anaerobic exercises. As we learn more about each form of exercise, we will also be presented with more opportunities to improve and widen our horizons in the xercise world. Flexibility exercises include the stretching of the muscles and joints to improve flexibility while aerobic exercises include walking, running or swimming to increase the cardiovascular endurance. Anaerobic exercises include more rigorous muscle exercises such as weight training or sprinting to increase the strength of the muscles. Physical exercise helps a person to maintain a healthy weight, healthy bones, muscles, and joints and promotes overall physiological and psychological well-being It also increases the strength of the immune system and may prevent the need for surgery or other invasive medical procedures down the road. Exercise has been proven to aid in proper brain function by increasing the flow of the blood and oxygen to the brain. It also increases the growth factor of nerve cells in the body by increasing the chemicals that are needed for cognition. The active breathing that takes place during exercise can help to increase a person's lung capacity and oxygen intake. This brings about a greater cardiac efficiency because the heart will do less work when it has to oxygenate the muscles. Conscious deep breathing during aerobic exercise will help to develop heart and lung efficiency. All of these things work together to promote further advantages to our overall health and to give us even greater opportunities down the road.

YOGA Yoga is a Sanscrit term meaning "union". It is an ancient spiritual practice that began in India thousands of years ago where it is still practiced as a great tradition. There are many forms of yoga such as Karma, Bhakti, Jnana and Raja, but in the West it has become more associated with various postures and fitness exercises which can eventually lead to a more advanced form of relaxation. Yoga is a practice which certainly adheres to the law of attraction in that its advocates develop greater and greater expertise and eventually become attracted to the most advanced forms of yoga. These more advanced forms are practiced in the form of deep meditation and the ultimate experience of Samadhi or Enlightenment. It is said that the energies which an advanced student obtains from yoga will eventually and spontaneously attract the experience of Enlightenment through their own inherent powers and this is the ultimate goal of yoga. As a way of achieving Enlightenment, yoga is considered to be an essential part of both Hinduism and Buddhism and has also spread to many other religions around the world. Traditional yogic techniques not only incorporate stretching and breathing exercises but typically include moral and ethical principles and a spiritual philosophy similar to that which is contained in the law of attraction itself. We call those energies toward ourselves which we meditate on everyday and this is basically an advanced application of the law of attraction. Eventually students may find themselves attracted to the specific teachings of a guru and may find themselves chanting specific mantras such as the sound "Om" which is considered by many enlightened masters to be the sacred sound of the universe. Many people now see yoga as a daily practice that is beneficial because it leads to an improved health, emotional balance, clarity of thought and a joy of life. Students of yoga may also be attracted to several breathing exercises and a stilling of the mind through the technique of meditation and this is merely a more focused aspect of the many yogic practices. MEDITATION Meditation is a specific element of yoga which generally involves the turning of a person's attention inward to the workings of their own mind and thoughts. It encompasses a lot of different spiritual practices but generally focuses on the mental activity and an achievement of internal peace. Many practitioners of meditation see it as a great way to become friendlier and healthier in their own lives. A derivative of meditation which is more commonly practiced in the Christian religion is that of contemplation where the mind is encouraged to reflect upon certain ideas so as to bring it into a more harmonious alignment with healthier attitudes and directions. An example of Christian contemplation might be the contemplation of the sufferings of Christ. Generally speaking, however, meditation tends to be a practice which focuses the mind on a single object or idea such as the breath or a sacred mantra. By practicing meditation, people become better at opening up to the powers of the divine and these powers become even more attractive as they develop inside each person.

powers of the divine and these powers become even more attractive as they develop inside each person.

The law of attraction is a profound truth that has been passed down to us through the teachings of the Buddha and through numerous other spiritual traditions throughout history. It has been explained to us that our actions don't just have an effect in this life but in future lives and that this is the reason for our fortunes and our sorrows each minute. Even science has shown us that the power of attraction is extremely significant in every aspect of our lives and is akin to the very glue which holds the entire universe together. If we wish to harness the immense strength of this power of attraction, it can only be through our own will that we strive to change our direction and enter into a larger field of attraction which can bring a more comprehensive experience of joy and happiness in our lives. "As ye sow, so shall ye reap" is offered to us both as Christians and Buddhists alike, and Earl Nightengale has given us a modern wake-up call to this pervasive truth in his "Strange Secret" philosophy. He has aptly told us "We become what we think about" and indeed, this law of attraction is becoming more and more understood each day. As we advance forward and come to know the great powers that lie within our own consciousness we learn that they only need to be unlocked in order that they reach their fullest potential. Once this happens, the "Strange Secret" that Nightengale speaks of may no longer be a secret and there may be nothing strange about it to anyone.

4

My Working Creed.

I believe that the mind of Man contains the greatest of all forces—that Thought is one of the greatest manifestations of energy. I believe that the man who understands the use of Thought-force can make of himself practically what he will. I believe that not only is one's body subject to the control of the mind, but that, also, one may change environment, "luck," circumstances, by positive thought taking the place of negative. I know that the "I Can and I Will" attitude will carry one forward to Success that will seem miraculous to the man on the "I Can't" plane. I believe that "thoughts are things," and that the Law of Attraction in the thought world will draw to one just what he desires or fears. I believe in the gospel of work—in "hustling." I believe in the I do, as well as the I am. I know that the man who will take advantage of the Power of the Mind, and who will manifest that power in action, will go forward to Success as surely and as steadily as the arrow from the bow of the skilled archer. I believe in the Brotherhood of Man. I believe in being Kind.I believe in everyone minding his own business—and allowing everyone else the same privilege. I believe that we have no right to condemn—"let him who is without sin cast the first stone." I believe that he who Hates is an assassin; that he who Covets is a thief; that he who Lusts is an adulterer; that the gist of a crime is in its desire. Seeing this—looking into our own hearts—how can we condemn? I believe that Evil is but Ignorance. I believe that "to know all is to forgive all." I believe that there is good in every man; let us help him to manifest it. I believe in the absolute equality of the Man and the Woman—sometimes I think that the odds are slightly in favor of the Woman. I believe in the sacredness of Sex—but I also believe that Sex manifests on the Spiritual and Mental planes as well as on the Physical. And I believe that to the pure all things are pure. I believe that man is immortal—that the Real Self is Spirit, which uses mind and body as its tools, and manifests itself according to the fitness of the tools. I believe that Man is rapidly growing into a new plane of consciousness, in which he will know himself as he is—will recognize the I am—the Something Within. I believe that there is an Infinite Power in, and of, all things. I believe that, although today we have but the faintest idea of that Power, still we will steadily grow to comprehend it more fully—will get in closer touch with it. Even now we have momentary glimpses of its existence—a momentary consciousness of Oneness with the Absolute. I believe that the greatest happiness consists in maintaining toward the Absolute the attitude of the trusting child, who, feeling no doubt of the parent's love—no doubt of his wisdom—places his little hand in that of the parent, and says "Lead Thou me on.I believe that he who feels towards the Absolute, the trustfulness of the babe which places its little tired head close to the breast of the mother, will also be conscious of the tender answering pressure, as the babe is drawn just a little closer to the mother-heart. William Walker Atkinson.

5

Law of Attraction in the Thought World.

One great Law—Thought a manifestation of Energy—Thought Vibration—Vibrations of light and heat differ solely in rate of vibration—Human brain only instrument capable of registering thought-waves—Experiments in telepathy prove the law of thought-attraction— Like attracts like in the Thought-world—The wireless telegraphy of the mind—A field of energy with established laws. The Universe is governed by Law—one great Law. Its manifestations are multiform, but viewed from the Ultimate there is but one Law. We are familiar with some of its manifestations, but are almost totally ignorant of certain others. Still we are learning a little more every day—the veil is being gradually lifted. We speak learnedly of the Law of Gravitation, but ignore that equally wonderful manifestation, The Law of Attraction in the Thought World. We are familiar with that wonderful manifestation of Law which draws and holds together the atoms of which matter is composed—we recognize the power of the law that attracts bodies to the earth, that holds the circling worlds in their places, but we close our eyes to the mighty law that draws to us the things we desire or fear, that makes or mars our lives.When we come to see that Thought is a force—a manifestation of energy— having a magnet- like power of attraction, we will begin to understand the why and wherefore of many things that have heretofore seemed dark to us. There is no study that will so well repay the student for his time and trouble as the study of the workings of this mighty law of the world of Thought—the Law of Attraction. When we think we send out vibrations of a fine ethereal substance, which are as real as the vibrations manifesting light, heat, electricity, magnetism. That these vibrations are not evident to our five senses is no proof that they do not exist. A powerful magnet will send out vibrations and exert a force sufficient to attract to itself a piece of steel weighing a hundred pounds, but we can neither see, taste, smell, hear nor feel the mighty force. These thought vibrations, likewise, cannot be seen, tasted, smelled, heard nor felt in the ordinary way; although it is true there are on record cases of persons peculiarly sensitive to psychic impressions who have perceived powerful thought-waves, and very many of us can testify that we have distinctly felt the thought vibrations of others, both whilst in the presence of the sender and at a distance. Telepathy and its kindred phenomena are not idle dreams. Light and heat are manifested by vibrations of a far lower intensity than those of Thought, but the difference is solely in the rate of vibration. The annals of science throw an interesting light upon this question. Prof. Elisha Gray, an eminent scientist, says in his little book, "The Miracles of Nature": "There is much food for speculation in the thought that there exist sound-waves that no human ear can hear, and color-waves of light that no eye can see. The long, dark, soundless space between 40,000 and 400,000,000,000,000 vibrations per second, and the infinity of range beyond 700,000,000,000,000 vibrations per second, where light ceases, in the universe of motion, makes it possible to indulge in speculation." M. M. Williams, in his work entitled "Short Chapters in Science," says: "There is no gradation between the most rapid undulations or tremblings that produce our sensation of sound, and the slowest of those which give rise to our sensations of gentlest warmth. There is a huge gap between them, wide enough to include another world of motion, all lying between our world of sound and our world of heat and light; and there is no good reason whatever for supposing that matter is incapable of such intermediate activity, or that such activity may not give rise to intermediate sensations, provided there are organs for taking up and sensifying their movements." I cite the above authorities merely to give you food for thought, not to attempt to demonstrate to you the fact that thought vibrations exist. The last-named fact has been fully established to the satisfaction of numerous investigators of the subject, and a little reflection will show you that it coincides with your own experiences. We often hear repeated the well-known Mental Science statement, "Thoughts are Things," and we say these words over without consciously realizing just what is the meaning of the statement. If we fully comprehended the truth of the statement and the natural consequences of the truth back of it, we should understand many things which have appeared dark to us, and would be able to use the wonderful power, Thought Force, just as we use any other manifestation of Energy. As I have said, when we think we set into motion vibrations of a very high degree, "but just as real as the vibrations of light, heat, sound, electricity." And when we understand the laws governing the production and transmission of these vibrations we will be able to use them in our daily life, just as we do the better known forms of energy. That we cannot see, hear, weigh or measure these vibrations is no proof that they do not exist. There exist waves of sound which no human ear can hear, although some of these are undoubtedly registered by the ear of some of the insects, and others are caught by delicate scientific instruments invented by man; yet there is a great gap between the sounds registered by the most delicate instrument and the limit which man's mind, reasoning by analogy, knows to be the boundary line between sound -waves and some other forms of vibration. And there are light waves which the eye of man does not register, some of Chapter I. The Law of Attraction in the Thought World. 5 which may be detected by more delicate instruments, and many more so fine that the instrument has not yet been invented which will detect them, although improvements are being made every year and the unexplored field gradually lessened. As new instruments are invented, new vibrations are registered by them— and yet the vibrations were just as real before the invention of the instrument as afterward. Supposing that we had no instruments to register magnetism— one might be justified in denying the existence of that mighty force, because it could not be tasted, felt, smelt, heard, seen, weighed or measured. And yet the mighty magnet would still send out waves of force sufficient to draw to it pieces of steel weighing hundreds of pounds. Each form of vibration requires its own form of instrument for registration. At present the human brain seems to be the only instrument capable of registering thought waves, although occultists say that in this century scientists will invent apparatus sufficiently delicate to catch and register such impressions. And from present indications it looks as if the invention named might be expected at any time. The demand exists and undoubtedly will be soon supplied. But to those who have experimented along the lines of practical telepathy no further proof is required than the results of their own experiments. We are sending out thoughts of greater or less intensity all the time, and we are reaping the results of such thoughts. Not only do our thought -waves influence ourselves and others, but they have a drawing power—they attract to us the thoughts of others, things, circumstances, people, "luck," in accord with the character of the thought uppermost in our minds. Thoughts of Love will attract to us the Love of others; circumstances and surroundings in accord with the thought; people who are of like thought. Thoughts of Anger, Hate, Envy, Malice and Jealousy will draw to us the foul brood of kindred thoughts emanating from the minds of others; circumstances in which we will be called upon to manifest these vile thoughts and will receive them in turn from others; people who will manifest inharmony; and so on. Thought Vibration 6 A strong thought, or a thought long continued, will make us the center of attraction for the corresponding thought-waves of others. Like attracts like in the Thought World—as ye sow so shall ye reap. Birds of a feather flock together in the Thought World—curses like chickens come home to roost, and bring their friends with them. The man or woman who is filled with Love sees Love on all sides and attracts the Love of others. The man with Hate in his heart gets all the Hate he can stand. The man who thinks Fight generally runs up against all the Fight he wants before he gets through. And so it goes, each gets what he calls for over the wireless telegraphy of the Mind. The man who rises in the morning feeling "grumpy" usually manages to have the whole family in the same mood before the breakfast is over. The "nagging" woman generally finds enough to gratify her "nagging" propensity during the day. This matter of Thought Attraction is a serious one. When you stop to think of it you will see that a man really makes his own surroundings, although he blames others for it. I have known people who understood this law to hold a positive, calm thought and be absolutely unaffected by the inharmony surrounding them. They were like the vessel from which the oil had been poured on the troubled waters—they rested safely and calmly whilst the tempest raged around them. One is not at the mercy of the fitful storms of Thought after he has learned the workings of the Law. We have passed through the age of physical force on to the age of intellectual supremacy, and are now entering a new and almost unknown field, that of psychic power. This field of energy has its established laws, as well as have the others, and we should acquaint ourselves with them or we will be crowded to the wall as are the ignorant on the planes of effort. I will endeavor to make plain to you the great underlying principles of this new field of energy which is opening up before us, that you may be able to make use of this great power and apply it for legitimate and worthy purposes, just as men are using steam, electricity and other forms of energy today.

How thought-waves traverse the sea of Mind—The power possessed of reproducing themselves—Vibrations which affect us—Those which do not—Why?—We are what we have thought ourselves into being—The agency of others' thoughts in shaping our destiny— The working of the Law of Attraction illustrated by the Marconi wireless instruments—The Mind has many degrees of pitch—Positive thought—Negative thought—We are positive to some, negative to others—A knowledge of Mental Law can change us from negative to positive—More people on negative plane than on positive plane—Consequently more negative thought-vibrations—How to counterbalance them—Affirmations and auto-suggestions, and their uses—Establishing new mental attitudes—Development of the Will—A high tension not at all times desirable—Advantage of changing from positive to receptive, at will. Like a stone thrown into the water, thought produces ripples and waves which spread out over the great ocean of thought. There is this difference, however: the waves on the water move only on a level plane in all directions, whereas thought-waves move in all directions from a common center, just as do the rays from the sun. Just as we here on earth are surrounded by a great sea of air, so are we surrounded by a great sea of Mind. Our thought-waves move through this Chapter II. Thought-Waves And Their Process Of Reproduction. 9 vast mental ether, extending, however, in all directions, as I have explained, becoming somewhat lessened in intensity according to the distance traversed, because of the friction occasioned by the waves coming in contact with the great body of Mind surrounding us on all sides. These thought-waves have other qualities differing from the waves on the water. They have the property of reproducing themselves. In this respect they resemble sound-waves rather than waves upon the water. Just as a note of the violin will cause the thin glass to vibrate and "sing," so will a strong thought tend to awaken similar vibrations in minds attuned to receive it. Many of the "stray thoughts" which come to us are but reflections or answering vibrations to some strong thought sent out by another. But unless our minds are attuned to receive it, the thought will not likely affect us. If we are thinking high and great thoughts, our minds acquire a certain keynote corresponding to the character of the thoughts we have been thinking. And, this keynote once established, we will be apt to catch the vibrations of other minds keyed to the same thought. On the other hand, let us get into the habit of thinking thoughts of an opposite character, and we will soon be echoing the low order of thought emanating from the minds of the thousands thinking along the same lines. We are largely what we have thought ourselves into being, the balance being represented by the character of the suggestions and thought of others, which have reached us either directly by verbal suggestions or telepathically by means of such thought-waves. Our general mental attitude, however, determines the character of the thought-waves received from others as well as the thoughts emanating from ourselves. We receive only such thoughts as are in harmony with the general mental attitude held by ourselves; the thoughts not in harmony affecting us very little, as they awaken no response in us. The man who believes thoroughly in himself and maintains a positive strong mental attitude of Confidence and Determination is not likely to be affected by the adverse and negative thoughts of Discouragement Thought Vibration 10 and Failure emanating from the minds of other persons in whom these last qualities predominate. At the same time these negative thoughts, if they reach one whose mental attitude is pitched on a low key, deepen his negative state and add fuel to the fire which is consuming his strength, or, if you prefer this figure, serve to further smother the fire of his energy and activity. We attract to us the thoughts of others of the same order of thought. The man who thinks success will be apt to get into tune with the minds of others thinking likewise, and they will help him, and he them. The man who allows his mind to dwell constantly upon thoughts of failure brings himself into close touch with the minds of other "failure" people, and each will tend to pull the other down still more. The man who thinks that all is evil is apt to see much evil, and will be brought into contact with others who will seem to prove his theory. And the man who looks for good in everything and everybody will be likely to attract to himself the things and people corresponding to his thought. We generally see that for which we look. You will be able to carry this idea more clearly if you will think of the Marconi wireless instruments, which receive the vibrations only from the sending instrument which has been attuned to the same key, while other telegrams are passing through the air in near vicinity without affecting the instrument. The same law applies to the operations of thought. We receive only that which corresponds to our mental attunement. If we have been discouraged, we may rest assured that we have dropped into a negative key, and have been affected not only by our own thoughts but have also received the added depressing thoughts of similar character which are constantly being sent out from the minds of other unfortunates who have not yet learned the law of attraction in the thought world. And if we occasionally rise to heights of enthusiasm and energy, how quickly we feel the inflow of the courageous, daring, energetic, positive thoughts being sent out by the live men and women of the world. We recognize this without much trouble when we come in personal contact with people and feel their vibrations, Chapter II. Thought-Waves And Their Process Of Reproduction. 11 depressing or invigorating, as the case may be. But the same law operates when we are not in their presence, although less strongly. The mind has many degrees of pitch, ranging from the highest positive note to the lowest negative note, with many notes in between, varying in pitch according to their respective distance from the positive or negative extreme. When your mind is operating along positive lines you feel strong, buoyant, bright, cheerful, happy, confident and courageous, and are enabled to do your work well, to carry out your intentions, and progress on your road to Success. You send out strong positive thought, which affects others and causes them to co-operate with you or to follow your lead, according to their own mental keynote. When you are playing on the extreme negative end of the mental keyboard you feel depressed, weak, passive, dull, fearful, cowardly. And you find yourself unable to make progress or to succeed. And your effect upon others is practically nil. You are led by, rather than leading others, and are used as a human door-mat or football by more positive persons. In some persons the positive element seems to predominate; and in others the negative quality seems to be more in evidence. There are, of course, widely varying degrees of positiveness and negativeness, and b may be negative to a, while positive to c. When two people first meet there is generally a silent mental conflict in which their respective minds test their quality of positiveness, and fix their relative position toward each other. This process may be unconscious in many cases, but it occurs nevertheless. The adjustment is often automatic, but occasionally the struggle is so sharp— the opponents being so well matched—that the matter forces itself into the consciousness of the two people. Sometimes both parties are so much alike in their degrees of positiveness that they practically fail to come to terms, mentally; they never really are able to get along with each other, and they are either mutually repelled and separate or else stay together amid constant broils and wrangling. Thought Vibration 12 We are positive or negative to everyone with whom we have relations. We may be positive to our children, our employees and dependents, but we are at the same time negative to others to whom we occupy inferior positions, or whom we have allowed to assert themselves over us. Of course, something may occur and we will suddenly become more positive than the man or woman to whom we have heretofore been negative. We frequently see cases of this kind. And as the knowledge of these mental laws becomes more general we will see many more instances of persons asserting themselves and making use of their new-found power. But remember you possess the power to raise the keynote of your mind to a positive pitch by an effort of the will. And, of course, it is equally true that you may allow yourself to drop into a low, negative note by carelessness or a weak will. There are more people on the negative plane of thought than on the positive plane, and consequently there are more negative thought vibrations in operation in our mental atmosphere. But, happily for us, this is counterbalanced by the fact that a positive thought is infinitely more powerful than a negative one, and if by force of will we raise ourselves to a higher mental key we can shut out the depressing thoughts and may take up the vibrations corresponding with our changed mental attitude. This is one of the secrets of the affirmations and auto-suggestions used by the several schools of Mental Science and other New Thought cults. There is no particular merit in affirmations of themselves, but they serve a twofold purpose: (1) They tend to establish new mental attitudes within us and act wonderfully in the direction of character building—the science of making ourselves over. (2) They tend to raise the mental keynote so that we may get the benefit of the positive thought-waves of others on the same plane of thought. Whether or not we believe in them, we are constantly making affirmations. The man who asserts that he can and will do a thing—and asserts it earnestly— develops in himself the qualities conducive to the well doing of that thing, Chapter II. Thought-Waves And Their Process Of Reproduction. 13 and at the same time places his mind in the proper key to receive all the thought-waves likely to help him in the doing. If, on the other hand, one says and feels that he is going to fail, he will choke and smother the thoughts coming from his own subconscious mentality which are intended to help him, and at the same time will place himself in tune with the Failure—thought of the world—and there is plenty of the latter kind of thought around, I can tell you. Do not allow yourselves to be affected by the adverse and negative thoughts of those around you. Rise to the upper chambers of your mental dwelling, and key yourself up to a strong pitch, away above the vibrations on the lower planes of thought. Then you will not only be immune to their negative vibrations but will be in touch with the great body of strong positive thought coming from those of your own plane of development. My aim will be to direct and train you in the proper use of thought and will, that you may have yourself well in hand and may be able to strike the positive key at any moment you may feel it necessary. It is not necessary to strike the extreme note on all occasions. The better plan is to keep yourself in a comfortable key, without much strain, and to have the means at command whereby you can raise the pitch at once when occasion demands. By this knowledge you will not be at the mercy of the old automatic action of the mind, but may have it well under your own control. Development of the will is very much like the development of a muscle—a matter of practice and gradual improvement. At first it is apt to be tiresome, but at each trial one grows stronger until the new strength becomes real and permanent. Many of us have made ourselves positive under sudden calls or emergencies. We are in the habit of "bracing up" when occasion demands. But by intelligent practice you will be so much strengthened that your habitual state will be equal to your "bracing up" stage now, and then when you find it necessary to apply the spur you will be able to reach a stage not dreamed of at present. Thought Vibration 14 Do not understand me as advocating a high tension continuously. This is not at all desirable, not only because it is apt to be too much of a strain upon you but also because you will find it desirable to relieve the tension at times and become receptive that you may absorb impressions. It is well to be able to relax and assume a certain degree of receptiveness, knowing that you are always able to spring back to the more positive state at will. The habitually strongly positive man loses much enjoyment and recreation. Positive, you give out expressions; receptive, you take in impressions. Positive, you are a teacher; receptive, a pupil. It is not only a good thing to be a good teacher, but it is also very important to be a good listener at times.

6

Talk About The Mind.

Man has but one Mind—Functions along two lines of mental effort—Passive effort often result of vibratory impulses imparted in ages long past—Active effort new-born—Thought impulse and motion impulse result of Active effort—Active function creates, Passive function obeys orders and suggestions—Active function sends forth vibrations—The force of Habit—Appetency—The impulse of the Primal Cause—"Life-force"—Mental Culture and Mental Development, two different things—The amenability of the Mind to the Will— The Will the outward manifestation of the I am—The attraction of The Absolute—The real Man the master—Active and Passive functions but tools. Man has but one mind, but he has many mental faculties, each faculty being capable of functioning along two different lines of mental effort. There are no distinct dividing lines separating the two several functions of a faculty, but they shade into each other as do the colors of the spectrum. An Active effort of any faculty of the mind is the result of a direct impulse imparted at the time of the effort. A Passive effort of any faculty of the mind is the result of either a preceding Active effort of the same mind; an Active effort of another along the lines of suggestion; Thought Vibrations from the mind of another; Thought impulses from an ancestor, transmitted by the laws of heredity (including impulses transmitted from generation to Chapter III. A Talk About The Mind. 17 generation from the time of the original vibratory impulse imparted by the Primal Cause—which impulses gradually unfold, and unsheath, when the proper state of evolutionary development is reached). The Active effort is new-born—fresh from the mint, whilst the Passive effort is of less recent creation, and, in fact, is often the result of vibratory impulses imparted in ages long past. The Active effort makes its own way, brushing aside the impeding vines and kicking from its path the obstructing stones. The Passive effort travels along the beaten path. A thought-impulse, or motion-impulse, originally caused by an Active effort of faculty, may become by continued repetition, or habit, strictly automatic, the impulse given it by the repeated Active effort developing a strong momentum, which carries it on, along Passive lines, until stopped by another Active effort or its direction changed by the same cause. On the other hand, thought-impulses, or motion-impulses, continued along Passive lines may be terminated or corrected by an Active effort. The Active function creates, changes or destroys. The Passive function carries on the work given it by the Active function and obeys orders and suggestions. The Active function produces the thought-habit, or motion-habit, and imparts to it the vibrations which carry it on along the Passive lines thereafter. The Active function also has the power to send forth vibrations which neutralize the momentum of the thought-habit, or motion -habit; it also is able to launch a new thought -habit, or motion-habit, with stronger vibrations, which overcomes and absorbs the first thought, or motion, and substitutes the new one. All thought-impulses, or motion-impulses, once started on their errands, continue to vibrate along passive lines until corrected or terminated by subsequent impulses imparted by the Active function, or other controlling power. The continuance of the original impulse adds momentum and force to it, and renders its correction or termination more difficult. This explains that which is called "the force of habit." I think that this will be readily understood by those who have struggled to overcome a habit which had Thought Vibration 18 been easily acquired. The Law applies to good habits as well as bad. The moral is obvious. Several of the faculties of the mind often combine to produce a single manifestation. A task to be performed may call for the combined exercise of several faculties, some of which may manifest by Active effort and others by Passive effort. The meeting of new conditions—new problems—calls for the exercise of Active effort; whilst a familiar problem, or task, can be easily handled by the Passive effort without the assistance of his more enterprising brother. There is in Nature an instinctive tendency of living organisms to perform certain actions, the tendency of an organized body to seek that which satisfies the wants of its organism. This tendency is sometimes called Appetency. It is really a Passive mental impulse, originating with the impetus imparted by the Primal Cause, and transmitted along the lines of evolutionary development, gaining strength and power as it progresses. The impulse of the Primal Cause is assisted by the powerful upward attraction exerted by The Absolute. In plant life this tendency is plainly discernible, ranging from the lesser exhibitions in the lower types to the greater in the higher types. It is that which is generally spoken of as the "life force" in plants. It is, however, a manifestation of rudimentary mentation, functioning along the lines of Passive effort. In some of the higher forms of plant life there appears a faint color of independent "life action"—a faint indication of choice of volition. Writers on plant life relate many remarkable instances of this phenomenon. It is, undoubtedly, an exhibition of rudimentary Active mentation. In the lower animal kingdom a very high degree of Passive mental effort is found. And, varying in degree in the several families and species, a considerable amount of Active mentation is apparent. The lower animal undoubtedly possesses Reason only in a lesser degree than man, and, in fact, the display of volitional mentation exhibited by an intelligent animal is often nearly as high as that shown by the lower types of man or by a young child. Chapter III. A Talk About The Mind. 19 As a child, before birth, shows in its body the stages of the physical evolution of man, so does a child, before and after birth—until maturity— manifest the stages of the mental evolution of man. Man, the highest type of life yet produced, at least upon this planet, shows the highest form of Passive mentation, and also a much higher development of Active mentation than is seen in the lower animals, and yet the degrees of that power vary widely among the different races of men. Even among men of our race the different degrees of Active mentation are plainly noticeable; these degrees not depending by any means upon the amount of "culture," social position or educational advantages possessed by the individual. Mental Culture and Mental Development are two very different things. You have but to look around you to see the different stages of the development of Active mentation in man. The reasoning of many men is scarcely more than Passive mentation, exhibiting but little of the qualities of volitional thought. They prefer to let other men think for them. Active mentation tires them and they find the instinctive, automatic, Passive mental process much easier. Their minds work along the lines of least resistance. They are but little more than human sheep. Among the lower animals and the lower types of men Active mentation is largely confined to the grosser faculties—the more material plane; the higher mental faculties working along the instinctive, automatic lines of the Passive function. As the lower forms of life progressed in the evolutionary scale, they developed new faculties, which were latent within them. These faculties always manifested in the form of rudimentary

Passive functioning, and afterwards worked up, through higher Passive forms, until the Active functions were brought into play. The evolutionary process still continues, the invariable tendency being toward the goal of highly developed Active mentation. This evolutionary progress is caused by the vibratory impulse imparted by the Primal Cause, aided by the uplifting attraction of The Absolute. Thought Vibration 20 This law of evolution is still in progress, and man is beginning to develop new powers of mind, which, of course, are first manifesting themselves along the lines of Passive effort. Some men have developed these new faculties to a considerable degree, and it is possible that before long Man will be able to exercise them along the line of their Active functions. In fact, this power has already been attained by a few. This is the secret of the Oriental occultists, and of some of their Occidental brethren. The amenability of the mind to the Will can be increased by properly directed practice. That which we are in the habit of referring to as the "strengthening of the Will" is in reality the training of the mind to recognize and absorb the Power Within. The Will is strong enough; it does not need strengthening, but the mind needs to be trained to receive and act upon the suggestions of the Will. The Will is the outward manifestation of the I am. The Will current is flowing in full strength along the spiritual wires; but you must learn how to raise the trolley-pole to touch it before the mental car will move. This is a somewhat different idea from that which you have been in the habit of receiving from writers on the subject of Will Power, but it is correct, as you will demonstrate to your own satisfaction if you will follow up the subject by experiments along the proper lines. The attraction of The Absolute is drawing man upward, and the vibratory force of the Primal Impulse has not yet exhausted itself. The time of evolutionary development has come when man can help himself. The man who understands the Law can accomplish wonders by means of the development of the powers of the mind; whilst the man who turns his back upon the truth will suffer from his lack of knowledge of the Law. He who understands the laws of his mental being, develops his latent powers and uses them intelligently. He does not despise his Passive mental functions, but makes good use of them also, charges them with the duties for which they are best fitted, and is able to obtain wonderful results from their work, having mastered them and trained them to do the bidding of the Higher Self. When they fail to do their work properly he regulates them, Chapter III. A Talk About The Mind. 21 and his knowledge prevents him from meddling with them unintelligently, and thereby doing himself harm. He develops the faculties and powers latent within him and learns how to manifest them along the line of Active mentation as well as Passive. He knows that the real man within him is the master to whom both Active and Passive functions are but tools. He has banished Fear, and enjoys Freedom. He has found himself. He has learned the secret of the I am.

7
Mind Building

The Power of Man—Unconscious mind-building—The "I," the sovereign of the Mind—The Universal Will—The mastery of the Lower Self—The mental misgoverned by irresponsible faculties—The reestablishment of order in the mental kingdom—The first battle—The conquest of the Lesser Self by the Real Self—Affirmation and exercise. Man can build up his mind and make it what he wills. In fact, we are mind-building every hour of our lives, either consciously or unconsciously. The majority of us are doing the work unconsciously, but those who have seen a little below the surface of things have taken the matter in hand and have become conscious creators of their own mentality. They are no longer subject to the suggestions and influences of others but have become masters of themselves. They assert the "I," and compel obedience from the subordinate mental faculties. The "I" is the sovereign of the mind, and what we call will is the instrument of the "I." Of course, there is something back of this, and the Universal Will is higher than the Will of the Individual, but the latter is in much closer touch with the Universal Will than is generally supposed, and when one conquers the lower self, and asserts the "I," he becomes in close touch with the Universal Will and partakes largely of its wonderful power. The moment one asserts the "I," and Chapter IV. Mind Building. 23 "finds himself," he establishes a close connection between the Individual Will and the Universal Will. But before he is able to avail himself of the mighty power at his command, he must first effect the Mastery of the lower self. Think of the absurdity of Man claiming to manifest powers, when he is the slave of the lower parts of his mental being, which should be subordinate. Think of a man being the slave of his moods, passions, animal appetites and lower faculties, and at the same time trying to claim the benefits of the Will. Now, I am not preaching asceticism, which seems to me to be a confession of weakness. I am speaking of Self-Mastery—the assertion of the "I" over the subordinate parts of oneself. In the higher view of the subject, this "I" is the only real Self, and the rest is the non-self; but our space does not permit the discussion of this point, and we will use the word "self" as meaning the entire man. Before a man can assert the "I" in its full strength he must obtain the complete mastery of the subordinate parts of the self. All things are good when we learn to master them, but no thing is good when it masters us. Just so long as we allow the lower portions of the self to give us orders, we are slaves. It is only when the "I" mounts his throne and lifts the sceptre, that order is established and things assume their proper relation to each other. We are finding no fault with those who are swayed by their lower selves— they are in a lower grade of evolution, and will work up in time. But we are calling the attention of those who are ready, to the fact that the Sovereign must assert his will, and that "the subjects must obey. Orders must be given and carried out. Rebellion must be put down, and the rightful" authority insisted upon. And the time to do it is Now. You have been allowing your rebellious subjects to keep the King from his throne. You have been allowing the mental kingdom to be misgoverned by irresponsible faculties. You have been the slaves of Appetite, Unworthy Thoughts, Passion and Negativeness. The Will has been set aside and Low Desire has usurped the throne. It is time to re-establish order in the mental kingdom. Thought Vibration 24 You are able to assert the mastery over any emotion, appetite, passion or class of thoughts by the assertion of the Will. You can order Fear to go to the rear; Jealousy to leave your presence; Hate to depart from your sight; Anger to hide itself; Worry to cease troubling you; Uncontrolled Appetite and Passion to bow in submission and to become humble slaves instead of masters—all by the assertion of the "I." You may surround yourself with the glorious company of Courage, Love and Self-Control, by the same means. You may put down the rebellion and secure peace and order in your mental kingdom if you will but utter the mandate and insist upon its execution. Before you march forth to empire, you must establish the proper internal conditions—must show your ability to govern your own kingdom. The first battle is the conquest of the lesser self by the Real Self. Affirmation. I Am Asserting the Mastery of My Real Self. Repeat these words earnestly and positively during the day, at least once an hour, and particularly when you are confronted with conditions which tempt you to act on the lines of the lesser self instead of following the course dictated by the Real Self. In the moment of doubt and hesitation, say these words earnestly, and your way will be made clear to you. Repeat them several times after you retire and settle yourself to sleep. But be sure to back up the words with the thought inspiring them, and do not merely repeat them parrot-like. Form the mental image of the Real Self asserting its mastery over the lower planes of your mind—see the King on his Throne. You will become conscious of an influx of new thought, and things which have seemed hard for you will suddenly become much easier. You will feel that you have yourself well in hand, and that you are the master and not the slave. The thought you are holding will manifest itself in action, and you will steadily grow to become that which you have in mind. Chapter IV. Mind Building. 25 Exercise. Fix the mind firmly on the higher Self and draw inspiration from it when you feel led to yield to the promptings of the lower part of your nature. When you are tempted to burst into Anger—assert the "I," and your voice will drop. Anger is unworthy of the developed Self. When you feel vexed and cross, remember what you are, and rise above your feeling. When you feel Fearful, remember that the Real Self fears nothing, and assert Courage. When you feel Jealousy inciting, think of your higher nature, and laugh. And so on, asserting the Real Self and not allowing the things on the lower plane of mentality to disturb you. They are unworthy of you, and must be taught to keep their places. Do not allow these things to master you—they should be your subjects, not your masters. You must get away from this plane, and the only way to do so is to cut loose from these phases of thought which have been "running things" to suit themselves. You may have trouble at the start, but keep at it and you will have that satisfaction which comes only from conquering the lower parts of our nature. You have been a slave long enough—now is the time to free yourselves. If you will follow these exercises faithfully you will be a different being by the end of the year, and will look back with a pitying smile to your former condition. But it takes work. This is not child's play, but a task for earnest men and women. Will you make the effort?

8

The Secret of the Will.

The Will Power and its capability of being developed, disciplined, controlled and directed— Every man the possessor, potentially, of a strong will—The great power-house of the Universal Will Power—Will does not need training, but Mind does—Mind, the instrument— Mentally lazy people—Strong will follows strong desire—The price of attainment—The real test-The secret of the development of the Will—Auto-suggestion and exercise. While psychologists may differ in their theories regarding the nature of the Will, none deny its existence, nor question its power. All persons recognize the power of strong Will—all see how it may be used to overcome the greatest obstacles. But few realize that the Will may be developed and strengthened by intelligent practice. They feel that they could accomplish wonders if they had a strong Will, but instead of attempting to develop it, they content themselves with vain regrets. They sigh, but do nothing. Those who have investigated the subject closely know that Will Power, with all its latent possibilities and mighty powers, may be developed, disciplined, controlled and directed, just as may be any other of Nature's forces. It does not matter what theory you may entertain about the nature of the Will, you will obtain the results if you practice intelligently.Personally, I have a somewhat odd theory about the Will. I believe that every man has, potentially, a strong Will, and that all he has to do is to train his mind to make use of it. I think that in the higher regions of the mind of every man is a great store of Will Power awaiting his use. The Will current is running along the psychic wires, and all that it is necessary to do is to raise the mental trolley-pole and bring down the power for your use. And the supply is unlimited, for your little storage battery is connected with the great power house of the Universal Will Power, and the power is inexhaustible. Your Will does not need training—but your Mind does. The mind is the instrument and the supply of Will Power is proportionate to the fineness of the instrument through which it manifests. But you needn't accept this theory if you don't like it. This lesson will fit your theory as well as mine. He who has developed his mind so that it will allow the Will Power to manifest through it, has opened up wonderful possibilities for himself. Not only has he found a great power at his command, but he is able to bring into play, and use, faculties, talents and abilities of whose existence he has not dreamed. This secret of the Will is the magic key which opens all doors. The late Donald G. Mitchell once wrote: "Resolve is what makes a man manifest; not puny resolve, but crude determination; not errant purpose— but that strong and indefatigable will which treads down difficulties and danger, as a boy treads down the heaving frost-lands of winter; which kindles his eye and brain with a proud pulse-beat toward the unattainable. Will makes men giants." Many of us feel that if we would but exert our Will, we might accomplish wonders. But somehow we do not seem to want to take the trouble—at any rate, we do not get to the actual willing point. We put it off from time to time, and talk vaguely of "some day," but that some day never comes. We instinctively feel the power of the Will, but we haven't enough energy to exercise it, and so drift along with the tide, unless perhaps some friendly difficulty arises, some helpful obstacle appears in our path, or some kindly Thought Vibration 28 pain stirs us into action, in either of which cases we are compelled to assert our Will and thus begin to accomplish something. The trouble with us is that we do not want to do the thing enough to make us exert our Will Power. We don't want to hard enough. We are mentally lazy and of weak Desire. If you do not like the word Desire substitute for it the word "Aspiration." (Some people call the lower impulses Desires, and the higher, Aspirations—it's all a matter of words, take your choice.) That is the trouble. Let a man be in danger of losing his life—let a woman be in danger of losing a great love—and you will witness a startling exhibition of Will Power from an unexpected source. Let a woman's child be threatened with danger, and she will manifest a degree of Courage and Will that sweeps all before it. And yet the same woman will quail before a domineering husband, and will lack the Will to perform a simple task. A boy will do all sorts of work if he but considers it play, and yet he can scarcely force himself to cut a little fire-wood. Strong Will follows strong Desire. If you really want to do a thing very much, you can usually develop the Will Power to accomplish it. The trouble is that you have not really wanted to do these things, and yet you blame your Will. You say that you do want to do it, but if you stop to think you will see that you really want to do something else more than the thing in question. You are not willing to pay the price of attainment. Stop a moment and analyze this statement and apply it to your own case. You are mentally lazy—that's the trouble. Don't talk to me about not having enough Will. You have a great storehouse of Will awaiting your use, but you are too lazy to use it. Now, if you are really in earnest about this matter, get to work and first find out what you really want to do—then start to work and do it. Never mind about the Will Power—you'll find a full supply of that whenever you need it. The thing to do is to get to the point where you will resolve to Will. That's the real test—the resolving. Think of these things a little, and make up your mind whether or not you really want to be a Willer sufficiently hard to get to work.

Many excellent essays and books have been written on this subject, all of which agree regarding the greatness of Will Power, the most enthusiastic terms being used; but few have anything to say about how this power may be acquired by those who have it not, or who possess it in but a limited degree. Some have given exercises designed to "strengthen" the Will, which exercises really strengthen the Mind so that it is able to draw upon its store of power. But they have generally overlooked the fact that in auto-suggestion is to be found the secret of the development of the mind so that it may become the efficient instrument of the Will. Auto-Suggestion I Am Using My Will Power. Say these words several times earnestly and positively, immediately after finishing this article. Then repeat them frequently during the day, at least once an hour, and particularly when you meet something that calls for the exercise of Will Power. Also repeat them several times after you retire and settle yourself for sleep. Now, there is nothing in these words unless you back them up with the thought. In fact, the thought is "the whole thing," and the words only pegs upon which to hang the thought. So think of what you are saying, and mean, what you say. You must use Faith at the start, and use the words with a confident expectation of the result. Hold the steady thought that you are drawing on your storehouse of Will Power, and before long you will find that thought is taking form in action, and that your Will Power is manifesting itself. You will feel an influx of strength with each repetition of the words. You will find yourself overcoming difficulties and bad habits, and will be surprised at how things are being smoothed out for you. Exercise Perform at least one disagreeable task each day during the month. If there is any specially disagreeable task which you would like to shirk, that is the one for you to perform. This is not given you in order to make you Thought Vibration 30 self-sacrificing or meek, or anything of that sort—it is given you to exercise your Will. Anyone can do a pleasant thing cheerfully, but it takes Will to do the unpleasant thing cheerfully; and that is how you must do the work. It will prove a most valuable discipline to you. Try it for a month and you will see where it "comes in." If you shirk this exercise you had better stop right here and acknowledge that you do not want Will Power, and are content to stay where you are and remain a weakling.

9

How to Become Immune to Injurious Thought Attraction.

————❦————

The first thing to do—Fear thought—Strong expectancy a powerful magnet—The man who fears—How to overcome the habit of Fear—A waste of time to fight negative thought by denying it—The right mental attitude—Setting new vibrations in motion—The conquest of Fear the first important step—The positive will prevail. The first thing to do is to begin to "cut out" Fear and Worry. Fearthought is the cause of much unhappiness and many failures. You have been told this thing over and over again, but it will bear repeating. Fear is a habit of mind which has been fastened upon us by negative race-thought, but from which we may free ourselves by individual effort and perseverance. Strong expectancy is a powerful magnet. He of the strong, confident desire attracts to him the things best calculated to aid him—persons, things, circumstances, surroundings; if he desires them hopefully, trustfully, confidently, calmly. And, equally true, he who Fears a thing generally manages to start into operation forces which will cause the thing he feared to come upon him. Don't you see, the man who Fears really expects the feared thing, and in the eyes of the Law it is the same as if he really had wished for or desired it? The Law is operative in both cases—the principle is the same. How to Become Immune to Injurious Thought Attraction. 33 The best way to overcome the habit of Fear is to assume the mental attitude of Courage, just as the best way to get rid of darkness is to let in the light. It is a waste of time to fight a negative thought-habit by recognizing its force and trying to deny it out of existence by mighty efforts. The best, surest, easiest and quickest method is to assume the existence of the positive thought desired in its place; and by constantly dwelling upon the positive thought, manifest it into objective reality. Therefore, instead of repeating, "I'm not afraid," say boldly, "I am full of Courage," "I am Courageous." You must assert, "There's nothing to fear," which, although in the nature of a denial, simply denies the reality of the object causing fear rather than admitting the fear itself and then denying it. To overcome Fear, one should hold firmly to the mental attitude of Courage. He should think Courage, say Courage, act Courage. He should keep the mental picture of Courage before him all the time, until it becomes his normal mental attitude. Hold the ideal firmly before you and you will gradually grow to its attainment—the ideal will become manifest. Let the word "Courage" sink deeply into your mind, and then hold it firmly there until the mind fastens it in place. Think of yourself as being Courageous—see yourself as acting with Courage in trying situations. Realize that there is nothing to Fear—that Worry and Fear never helped anyone, and never will. Realize that Fear paralyzes effort, and that Courage promotes activity. The confident, fearless, expectant, "I Can and I Will" man is a mighty magnet. He attracts to himself just what is needed for his success. Things seem to come his way, and people say he is "lucky." Nonsense! "Luck" has nothing to do with it. It's all in the Mental Attitude. And the Mental Attitude of the "I Can't" or the "I'm Afraid" man also determines his measure of success. There's no mystery whatsoever about it. You have but to look about you to realize the truth of what I have said. Did you ever know a successful man who did not have the "I Can and I Will" thought strong within him? Why, he will walk all around the "I Can't" man, who has perhaps even more ability.

The first mental attitude brought to the surface latent qualities, as well as attracted help from outside; whilst the second mental attitude not only attracted "I Can't" people and things, but also kept the man's own powers from manifesting themselves. I have demonstrated the correctness of these views, and so have many others, and the number of people who know these things is growing every day. Don't waste your Thought-Force, but use it to advantage. Stop attracting to yourself failure, unhappiness, inharmony, sorrow—begin now and send out a current of bright, positive, happy thought. Let your prevailing thought be "I Can and I Will;" think "I Can and I Will;" dream "I Can and I Will;" say "I Can and I Will;" act "I Can and I Will." Live on the "I Can and I Will" plane, and before you are aware of it, you will feel the new vibrations manifesting themselves in action; will see them bring results; will be conscious of the new point of view; will realize that your own is coming to you. You will feel better, act better, see better, be better in every way, after you join the "I Can and I Will" brigade. Fear is the parent of Worry, Hate, Jealousy, Malice, Anger, Discontent, Failure and all the rest. The man who rids himself of Fear will find that the rest of the brood have disappeared. The only way to be Free is to get rid of Fear. Tear it out by the roots. I regard the conquest of Fear as the first important step to be taken by those who wish to master the application of Thought Force. So long as Fear masters you, you are in no condition to make progress in the realm of Thought, and I must insist that you start to work at once to get rid of this obstruction. You can do it—if you only go about it in earnest. And when you have ridded yourself of the vile thing, life will seem entirely different to you—you will feel happier, freer, stronger, more positive, and will be more successful in every undertaking of Life. Start in today, make up your mind that this intruder must go—do not compromise matters with him, but insist upon an absolute surrender on his part. You will find the task difficult at first, but each time you oppose him he will grow weaker, and you will be stronger. Shut off his nourishment—starve Chapter VI. How to Become Immune to Injurious Thought Attraction. 35 him to death—he cannot live in a thought—atmosphere of Fearlessness. So, start to fill your mind with good, strong, Fearless thoughts—keep yourself busy thinking Fearlessness, and Fear will die of his own accord. Fearlessness is positive—Fear is negative, and you may be sure that the positive will prevail. So long as Fear is around with his "but," "if," "suppose," "I'm afraid," "I can't," "what if," and all the rest of his cowardly suggestions, you will not be able to use your Thought Force to the best advantage. Once get him out of the way, you will have clear sailing, and every inch of thought-sail will catch the wind. He is a Jonah. Overboard with him! (The whale who swallows him will have my sympathy.) I advise that you start in to do some of the things which you feel you could do if you were not afraid to try. Start to work to do these things, affirming "Courage" all the way through, and you will be surprised to see how the changed mental attitude will clear away obstacles from your path, and will make things very much easier than you had anticipated. Exercises of this kind will develop you wonderfully, and you will be much gratified at the result of a little practice along these lines. There are many things before you awaiting accomplishment, which you can master if you will only throw aside the yoke of Fear—if you will only refuse to accept the race suggestion, and will boldly assert the "I" and its power. And the best way to vanquish Fear is to assert "Courage" and stop thinking of Fear. By this plan you will train the mind into new habits of thought, thus eradicating the old negative thoughts which have been pulling you down, and holding you back. Take the word "Courage" with you as your watchword and manifest it in action. Remember, the only thing to fear is Fear, and—well, don't even fear Fear, for he's a cowardly chap at the best, who will run if you show a brave front.

10

The Transmutation of Negative Thought.

Worry the child of Fear—The motive underlying action—The causes that result in Success— How Desire acts—Worry negative and death-producing—Desire and Ambition positive and life-producing—The transmutation of Worry—Getting into harmony with the right thought-waves—Setting in motion the Law of Attraction—Fear paralyzes Desire—Once rid of it, difficulty melts away—The working of a mighty Law—The things we worry about— Things adjust themselves—The storing-up of energy—Where are the feared things?— Better ways of overcoming objectionable thoughts than by fighting them. Worry is the child of Fear—if you kill out Fear, Worry will die for want of nourishment. This advice is very old, and yet it is always worthy of repetition, for it is a lesson of which we are greatly in need. Some people think that if we kill out Fear and Worry we will never be able to accomplish anything. I have read editorials in the great journals in which the writers held that without Worry one can never accomplish any of the great tasks of life, because Worry is necessary to stimulate interest and work. This is nonsense, no matter who utters it. Worry never helped one to accomplish anything; on the contrary, it stands in the way of accomplishment and attainment. The motive underlying action and "doing things" is Desire and Interest. If one earnestly desires a thing, he naturally becomes very much interested in its accomplishment, and is quick to seize upon anything likely to help him to gain the thing he wants. More than that, his mind starts up a work on the sub-conscious plane that brings into the field of consciousness many ideas of value and importance. Desire and Interest are the causes that result in success. Worry is not Desire. It is true that if one's surroundings and environments become intolerable, he is driven in desperation to some efforts that will result in throwing off the undesirable conditions and in the acquiring of those more in harmony with his desire. But this is only another form of Desire—the man desires something different from what he has; and when his desire becomes strong enough his entire interest is given to the task, he makes a mighty effort, and the change is accomplished. But it wasn't Worry that caused the effort. Worry could content itself with wringing its hands and moaning "Woe is me," and wearing its nerves to a frazzle, and accomplishing nothing. Desire acts differently. It grows stronger as the man's conditions become intolerable, and finally when he feels the hurt so strongly that he can't stand it any longer, he says, "I won't stand this any longer—I will make a change," and lo! then Desire springs into action. The man keeps on "wanting" a change the worst way (which is the best way) and his Interest and Attention being given to the task of deliverance, he begins to make things move. Worry never accomplished anything. Worry is negative and death producing. Desire and Ambition are positive and life producing. A man may worry himself to death and yet nothing will be accomplished, but let that man transmute his worry and discontent into Desire and Interest, coupled with a belief that he is able to make the change—the "I Can and I Will" idea— then something happens. Yes, Fear and Worry must go before we can do much. One must proceed to cast out these negative intruders, and replace them with Confidence and Hope. Transmute Worry into keen Desire. Then you will find that Interest is awakened, and you will begin to think things of interest to you. Thoughts will come to you from the great reserve stock in your mind and you will start to manifest them in action. Moreover you will be placing yourself in harmony with similar thoughts of others, and will draw to you aid and assistance from the great volume of thought waves with which the world is filled. One draws to himself thought waves corresponding in character with the nature of the prevailing thoughts in his own mind—his mental attitude. Then again he begins to set into motion the great Law of Attraction, whereby he draws to him others likely to help him, and is, in turn, attracted to others who can aid him. This Law of Attraction is no joke, no metaphysical absurdity, but is a great live working principle of Nature, as anyone may learn by experimenting and observing. To succeed in anything you must want it very much—Desire must be in evidence in order to attract. The man of weak desires attracts very little to himself. The stronger the Desire the greater the force set into motion. You must want a thing hard enough before you can get it. You must want it more than you do the things around you, and you must be prepared to pay the price for it. The price is the throwing overboard of certain lesser desires that stand in the way of the accomplishment of the greater one. Comfort, ease, leisure, amusements, and many other things may have to go (not always, though). It all depends on what you want. As a rule, the greater the thing desired, the greater the price to be paid for it. Nature believes in adequate compensation. But if you really Desire a thing in earnest, you will pay the price without question; for the Desire will dwarf the importance of the other things. You say that you want a thing very much, and are doing everything possible toward its attainment? Pshaw! you are only playing Desire. Do you want the thing as much as a prisoner wants freedom—as much as a dying man wants life? Look at the almost miraculous things accomplished by prisoners desiring freedom. Look how they work through steel plates and stone walls with a bit of stone. Is your desire as strong as that? Do you work for the desired thing as if your life depended upon it? Nonsense! you don't know what Desire is. I tell you if a man wants a thing as much as the prisoner wants freedom, or as much as a strongly vital man wants life, then that man will be able to sweep away obstacles and impediments apparently immovable. The key to attainment is Desire, Confidence, and Will. This key will open many doors. Fear paralyzes Desire—it scares the life out of it. You must get rid of Fear. There have been times in my life when Fear would get hold of me and take a good, firm grip on my vitals, and I would lose all hope; all interest; all ambition; all desire. But, thank the Lord, I have always managed to throw off the grip of the monster and face my difficulty like a man; and lo! things would seem to be straightened out for me somehow. Either the difficulty would melt away, or I would be given means to overcome it, or get around, or under or over it. It is strange how this works. No matter how great is the difficulty, when we finally face it with courage and confidence in ourselves, we seem to pull through somehow, and then we begin to wonder what we were scared about. This is not a mere fancy, it is the working of a mighty law, which we do not as yet fully understand, but which we may prove at any time. People often ask: "It's all very well for you New Thought people to say 'Don't worry,' but what's a person to do when he thinks of all the possible things ahead of him, which might upset him and his plans?" Well, all that I can say is that the man is foolish to bother about thinking of troubles to come at some time in the future. The majority of things that we worry about don't come to pass at all; a large proportion of the others come in a milder form than we had anticipated, and there are always other things which come at the same time which help us to overcome the trouble. The future holds in store for us not only difficulties to be overcome, but also agents to help us in overcoming the difficulties. Things adjust themselves. We are prepared for any trouble which may come upon us, and when the time comes we somehow find ourselves able to meet it. God not only tempers the wind to the shorn lamb, but He also tempers the shorn lamb to the wind. The wind and the shearing do not come together; there is usually enough time for the amb to get seasoned, and then he generally grows new wool before the cold blast comes. It has been well said that nine-tenths of the worries are over things which never come to pass, and that the other tenth is over things of little or no account. So what's the use in using up all your reserve force in fretting over future troubles, if this be so? Better wait until your troubles really come before you worry. You will find that by this storing up of energy you will be able to meet about any sort of trouble that comes your way. What is it that uses up all the energy in the average man or woman, anyway? Is it the real overcoming of difficulties, or the worrying about impending troubles? It's always "Tomorrow, tomorrow," and yet tomorrow never comes just as we feared it would. Tomorrow is all right; it carries in its grip good things as well as troubles. Bless my soul, when I sit down and think over the things which I once feared might possibly descend upon me, I laugh! Where are those feared things now? I don't know—have almost forgotten that I ever feared them. You do not need to fight Worry—that isn't the way to overcome the habit. Just practice concentration, and then learn to concentrate upon something right before you, and you will find that the worry thought has vanished. The mind can think of but one thing at a time, and if you concentrate upon a bright thing, the other thing will fade away. There are better ways of overcoming objectionable thoughts than by fighting them. Learn to concentrate upon thoughts of an opposite character, and you will have solved the problem. When the mind is full of worry thoughts, it cannot find time to work out plans to benefit you. But when you have concentrated upon bright, helpful thoughts, you will discover that it will start to work subconsciously; and when the time comes you will find all sorts of plans and methods by which you will be able to meet the demands upon you. Keep your mental attitude right, and all things will be added unto you. There's no sense in worrying; nothing has ever been gained by it, and nothing ever will be. Bright) cheerful and happy thoughts attract bright, cheerful and happy things to us—worry drives them away. Cultivate the right mental attitude.

11

The Law of Mental Control.

Thoughts either faithful servants or tyrannical masters—Some of our best mental work performed for us when our conscious mentality is at rest—The key to the mystery—The man who understands how to run his mental engine—"Slowing down" the Mind. Your thoughts are either faithful servants or tyrannical masters—just as you allow them to be. You have the say about it; take your choice. They will either go about your work under direction of the firm will, doing it the best they know how, not only in your waking hours, but when you are asleep—some of our best mental work being performed for us when our conscious mentality is at rest, as is evidenced by the fact that when the morning comes we find troublesome problems have been worked out for us during the night, after we had dismissed them from our minds—apparently; or they will ride all over us and make us their slaves if we are foolish enough to allow them to do so. More than half the people of the world are slaves of every vagrant thought which may see fit to torment them. Your mind is given you for your good and for your own use—not to use you. There are very few people who seem to realize this and who understand the art of managing the mind. The key to the mystery is Concentration. A little practice will develop within every man the power to use the mental Chapter VIII. The Law of Mental Control. 43 machine properly. When you have some mental work to do concentrate upon it to the exclusion of everything else, and you will find that the mind will get right down to business-to the work at hand-and matters will be cleared up in no time. There is an absence of friction, and all waste motion or lost power is obviated. Every pound of energy is put to use, and every revolution of the mental driving—wheel counts for something. It pays to be able to be a competent mental engineer. And the man who understands how to run his mental engine knows that one of the important things is to be able to stop it when the work has been done. He does not keep putting coal in the furnace, and maintaining a high pressure after the work is finished, or when the day's portion of the work has been done, and the fires should be banked until the next day. Some people act as if the engine should be kept running whether there was any work to be done or not, and then they complain if it gets worn out and wobbles and needs repairing. These mental engines are fine machines, and need intelligent care. To those who are acquainted with the laws of mental control it seems absurd for one to lie awake at night fretting about the problems of the day, or more often, of the morrow. It is just as easy to slow down the mind as it is to slow down an engine, and thousands of people are learning to do this in these days of New Thought. The best way to do it is to think of something else—as far different from the obtruding thought as possible. There is no use fighting an objectionable thought with the purpose of "downing" it; that is a great waste of energy, and the more you keep on saying, "I won't think of this thing!" the more it keeps on coming into your mind, for you are holding it there for the purpose of hitting it. Let it go; don't give it another thought; fix the mind on something entirely different, and keep the attention there by an effort of the will. A little practice will do much for you in this direction. There is only room for one thing at a time in the focus of attention; so put all your attention upon one thought, and the others will sneak off. Try it for yourself.

12

Asserting the Life-Force

❦

A general awakening needed—Let Life flow through us, manifesting in thought, word, deed—The expression of conscious life—Affirmation and Exercise. I have spoken to you of the advantage of getting rid of Fear. Now I wish to put life into you. Many of you have been going along as if you were dead— no ambition—no energy—no vitality—no interest—no life. This will never do. You are stagnating. Wake up and display a few signs of life! This is not the place in which you can stalk around like a living corpse—this is the place for wide-awake, active, live people, and a good general awakening is what is needed; although it would take nothing less than a blast from Gabriel's trumpet to awaken some of the people who are stalking around thinking that they are alive, but who are really dead to all that makes life worth while. We must let Life flow through us, and allow it to express itself naturally. Do not let the little worries of life, or the big ones either, depress you and cause you to lose your vitality. Assert the Life Force within you, and manifest it in every thought, act and deed, and before long you will be exhilarated and fairly bubbling over with vitality and energy. Put a little life into your work—into your pleasures—into yourself. Stop doing things in a half-hearted way, and begin to take an interest in what you are doing, saying and thinking. It is astonishing how much interest we may find in the ordinary things of life, if we will only wake up. There are interesting things all around us—interesting events occurring every moment—but we will not be aware of them unless we assert our life force and begin to actually live instead of merely existing. No man or woman ever amounted to anything unless he or she put life into the tasks of everyday life—the acts—the thoughts. What the world needs is live men and women. Just look into the eyes of the people whom you meet, and see how few of them are really alive. The most of them lack that expression of conscious life which distinguishes the man who lives from the one who simply exists. I want you to acquire this sense of conscious life so that you may manifest it in your life and show what Mental Science has done for you. I want you to get to work today and begin to make yourselves over according to the latest pattern. You can do this if you will only take the proper interest in the task. Affirmation and Exercise "I Am Alive." Fix in your mind the thought that the "I" within you is very much alive and that you are manifesting life fully, mentally and physically. And keep this thought there, aiding yourself with constant repetitions of the watchword. Don't let the thought escape you, but keep pushing it back into the mind. Keep it before the mental vision as much as possible. Repeat the watchword when you awaken in the morning—say it when you retire at night. And say it at meal times, and whenever else you can during the day—at least once an hour. Form the mental picture of yourself as filled with Life and Energy. Live up to it as far as possible. When you start in to perform a task say "I Am Alive" and mix up as much life as possible in the task. If you find yourself feeling depressed, say "I Am Alive," and then take a few deep breaths, and with each inhalation let the mind hold the thought that you are breathing in Strength and Life, and as you exhale, hold the thought that you are breathing Thought Vibration 46 out all the old, dead, negative conditions and are glad to get rid of them. Then finish up with an earnest, vigorous affirmation: "I Am Alive," and mean it when you say it, too. And let your thoughts take form in action. Don't rest content with merely saying that you are alive, but prove it with your acts. Take an interest in doing things, and don't go around "mooning" or day-dreaming. Get down to business, and live.

13

Training the Habit-Mind.

The sub-conscious mind—Importance of transmitting proper impulses—Automatic habits—"Which of these two things shall I do?"—Forming a new habit—Breaking an old one—The "just-once" idea—The Mind a piece of paper—Mental creases. Professor William James, the well-known teacher of, and writer upon Psychology, very truly says: "The great thing in all education is to make our nervous system our ally instead of our enemy. For this we must make automatic and habitual, as early as possible, as many useful actions as we can, and as carefully guard against growing into ways that are likely to be disadvantageous. In the acquisition of a new habit, or the leaving off of an old one, we must take care to launch ourselves with as strong and decided initiative as possible. Never suffer an exception to occur until the new habit is securely rooted in your life. Seize the very first possible opportunity to act on every resolution you make and on every emotional prompting you may experience, in the direction of the habits you aspire to gain." This advice is along the lines familiar to all students of Mental Science, but it states the matter more plainly than the majority of us have done. It impresses upon us the importance of passing on to the subconscious mind the proper impulses, so that they will become automatic and "second nature." Our subconscious mentality is a great store house for all sorts of suggestions from ourselves and others, and, as it is the "habit-mind," we must be careful to send it the proper material from which it may make habits. If we get into the habit of doing certain things, we may be sure that the subconscious mentality will make it easier for us to do just the same thing over and over again, easier each time, until finally we are firmly bound with the ropes and chains of the habit, and find it more or less difficult, sometimes almost impossible, to free ourselves from the hateful thing. We should cultivate good habits against the hour of need. The time will come when we will be required to put forth our best efforts, and it rests with us today whether that hour of need shall find us doing the proper thing automatically and almost without thought, or struggling to do it bound down and hindered with the chains of things opposed to that which we desire at that moment. We must be on guard at all times to prevent the forming of undesirable habits. There may be no special harm in doing a certain thing today, or perhaps again tomorrow, but there may be much harm in setting up the habit of doing that particular thing. If you are confronted with the question: "Which of these two things should I do?" the best answer is: "I will do that which I would like to become a habit with me." In forming a new habit, or in breaking an old one, we should throw ourselves into the task with as much enthusiasm as possible, in order to gain the most ground before the energy expends itself when it meets with friction from the opposing habits already formed. We should start in by making as strong an impression as possible upon the subconscious mentality. Then we should be constantly on guard against temptations to break the new resolution "just this once." This "just once" idea kills off more good resolutions than any other one cause. The moment you yield "just this once," you introduce the thin edge of the wedge that will, in the end, split your resolution into pieces.

Equally important is the fact that each time you resist temptation the stronger does your resolution become. Act upon your resolution as early and as often as possible, as with every manifestation of thought in action, the stronger does it become. You are adding to the strength of your original resolution every time you back it up with action. The mind has been likened to a piece of paper that has been folded. Ever afterwards it has a tendency to fold in the same crease—unless we make a new crease or fold, when it will follow the last lines. And the creases are habits—every time we make one it is so much easier for the mind to fold along the same crease afterward. Let us make our mental creases in the right direction.

14

The Psychology Of Emotion.

Emotions dependent largely upon habit—May be repressed, increased, developed, changed—When to master an undesirable emotion—Jealousy—Its growth—Rage—The habit of feeling and acting "mean"—Worry—Continued thought manifests in action— "Fault-finding"—The chronic "nagger"—Negative emotions and their recurrence—How to choke out these habits. One is apt to think of the emotions as independent from habit. We easily may think of one acquiring habits of action, and even of thinking, but we are apt to regard the emotions as something connected with "feeling" and quite divorced from intellectual effort. Yet, notwithstanding the distinction between the two, both are dependent largely upon habit, and one may repress, increase, develop, and change one's emotions, just as one may regulate habits of action and lines of thought. It is an axiom of psychology that "Emotions deepen by repetition." If a person allows a state of feeling to thoroughly take possession of him, he will find it easier to yield to the same emotion the second time, and so on, until the particular emotion or feeling becomes second nature to him. If an undesirable emotion shows itself inclined to take up a permanent abode with you, you had better start to work to get rid of it, or at least to master it. Chapter XI. The Psychology Of Emotion. 53 And the best time to do this is at the start; for each repetition renders the habit more firmly intrenched, and the task of dislodging it more difficult. Were you ever jealous? If so, you will remember how insidious was its first approach, how subtly it whispered hateful suggestions into your willing ear, and how gradually it followed up such suggestions, until, finally you began to see green, (Jealousy has an effect upon the bile, and causes it to poison the blood. This is why the idea of green is always associated with it.) Then you will remember how the thing seemed to grow, taking possession of you until you scarcely could shake it off. You found it much easier to become jealous the next time. It seemed to bring before you all sorts of objects apparently justifying your suspicions and feeling. Everything began to look green—the green -eyed monster waxed fat. And so it is with every feeling or emotion. If you give way to a fit of rage, you will find it easier to become angry the next time, on less provocation. The habit of feeling and acting "mean" does not take long to firmly settle itself in its new home if encouraged. Worry is a great habit for growing and waxing fat. People start by worrying about big things, and then begin to worry and fret about some smaller thing. And then the merest trifle worries and distresses them. They imagine that all sorts of evil things are about to befall them. If they start on a journey they are certain there is going to be a wreck. If a telegram comes, it is sure to contain some dreadful tidings. If a child seems a little quiet, the worrying mother is positive it is going to fall ill and die. If the husband seems thoughtful, as he revolves some business plan in his mind, then the good wife is convinced that he is beginning to cease to love her, and indulges in a crying spell. And so it goes—worry, worry, worry—each indulgence making the habit more at home. After a while the continued thought shows itself in action. Not only is the mind poisoned by the blue thoughts, but the forehead shows deep lines between the eyebrows, and the voice takes on that whining, rasping tone so common among worry-burdened people.

The condition of mind known as "fault-finding" is another emotion that grows fat with exercise. First, fault is found with this thing, then with that, and finally with everything. The person becomes a chronic "nagger"—a burden to friends and relatives, and a thing to be avoided by outsiders. Women make the greatest naggers. Not because men are any better, but simply because a man nagger is apt to have the habit knocked out of him by other men who will not stand his nonsense—he finds that he is making things too hot for himself, and he reforms; while a woman has more of a chance to indulge in the habit. But this nagging is all a matter of habit. It grows from small beginnings, and each time it is indulged in it throws out another root, branch, or tendril, and fastens itself the closer to the one who has given it soil in which to grow. Envy, uncharitableness, gossip, scandal-mongering, are all habits of this kind. The seeds are in every human breast, and only need good soil and a little watering to become lusty and strong. Each time you give way to one of these negative emotions, the easier do you make it for a recurrence of the same thing, or similar ones. Sometimes by encouraging one unworthy emotion, you find that you have given room for the growth of a whole family of these mental weeds. Now, this is not a good old orthodox preachment against the sin of bad thoughts. It is merely a calling of your attention to the law underlying the psychology of emotions. Nothing new about it—old as the hills—so old that many of us have forgotten all about it. If you wish to manifest these constantly disagreeable and unpleasant traits, and to suffer the unhappiness that comes from them, by all means do so—that is your own business, and privilege. It's none of mine, and I am not preaching at you—it keeps me busy minding my own business and keeping an eye on my own undesirable habits and actions. I am merely telling you the law regarding the matter, and you may do the rest. If you wish to choke out these habits, there are two ways open to you. First, whenever you find yourself indulging in a negative thought or feeling, take right hold of it and Chapter XI. The Psychology Of Emotion. 55 say to it firmly, and vigorously, "Get out!" It won't like this at first, and will bridle up, curve its back and snarl like an offended cat. But never mind—just say "Scat" to it. The next time it will not be so confident and aggressive—it will have manifested a little of the fear-habit. Each time you repress and choke out a tendency of this kind, the weaker it will become, and the stronger will your will be. Professor James says: "Refuse to express a passion, and it dies. Count ten before venting your anger, and its occasion seems ridiculous. Whistling to keep up courage is no mere figure of speech. On the other hand, sit all day in a moping posture, sigh, and reply to everything with a dismal voice, and your melancholy lingers. There is no more valuable precept in moral education than this, as all who have experience know: if we wish to conquer emotional tendencies in ourselves, we must assiduously, and in the first instance, cold-bloodedly, go through the outward movements of those contrary dispositions which we prefer to cultivate. ... Smooth the brow, brighten the eye, contract the dorsal rather than the ventral aspect of the frame, and speak in a major key, pass the genial compliment, and your heart must be frigid indeed if it does not gradually thaw.

15

Developing New Brain-Cells.

Undesirable states of feeling—We are not the creatures of our emotions—The majority of the race so governed to a great degree—Man the real master of his emotions—The development of new brain -cells—The disuse of old brain-cells with undesirable manifestations—The brain, the organ and instrument of the Mind—Our tendencies, temperaments and predispositions—The millions of unused brain-cells—Mental attitudes acquired or discarded at will—The mind clears the way for thoughts good for the individual, interposes resistance to those which are harmful—One positive thought will counteract a number of negative thoughts—"Holding the thought"—How to cultivate a certain habit of action—Ridding oneself of a mental trait. I have spoken of the plan of getting rid of undesirable states of feeling by driving them out. But a far better way is to cultivate the feeling or emotion directly opposed to the one you wish to eradicate. We are very apt to regard ourselves as the creatures of our emotions and feelings, and to fancy that these feelings and emotions are "we." But such is far from being the truth. It is true that the majority of the race are slaves of their emotions and feelings, and are governed by them to a great degree. They think that feelings are things that rule one and from which one cannot free himself, and so they cease to rebel. They yield to the feeling Chapter XII. Developing New Brain-Cells. 57 without question, although they may know that the emotion or mental trait is calculated to injure them, and to bring unhappiness and failure instead of happiness and success. They say "we are made that way," and let it go at that. The new Psychology is teaching the people better things. It tells them that they are masters of their emotions and feelings, instead of being their slaves. It tells them that brain-cells may be developed that will manifest along desirable lines, and that the old brain-cells that have been manifesting so unpleasantly may be placed on the retired list, and allowed to atrophy from want of use. People may make themselves over, and change their entire natures. This is not mere idle theory, but is a working fact which has been demonstrated by thousands of people, and which is coming more and more before the attention of the race. No matter what theory of mind we entertain, we must admit that the brain is the organ and instrument of the mind, in our present state of existence, at least, and that the brain must be considered in this matter. The brain is like a wonderful musical instrument, having millions of keys, upon which we may play innumerable combinations of sounds. We come into the world with certain tendencies, temperaments, and predispositions. We may account for these tendencies by heredity, or we may account for them upon theories of pre-existence, but the facts remain the same. Certain keys seem to respond to our touch more easily than others. Certain notes seem to sound forth as the current of circumstances sweeps over the strings. And certain other notes are less easily vibrated. But we find that if we but make an effort of the will to restrain the utterance of some of these easily sounded strings, they will grow more difficult to sound, and less liable to be stirred by the passing breeze. And if we will pay attention to some of the other strings that have not been giving forth a clear tone, we will soon get them in good working order; their notes will chime forth clear and vibrant, and will drown the less pleasant sounds. We have millions of unused brain-cells awaiting our cultivation. We are using but a few of them, and some of these we are working to death. We Thought Vibration 58 are able to give some of these cells a rest, by using other cells. The brain may be trained and cultivated in a manner incredible to one who has not looked into the subject. Mental attitudes may be acquired and cultivated, changed and discarded, at will. There is no longer any excuse for people manifesting unpleasant and harmful mental states. We have the remedy in our own hands. We acquire habits of thought, feeling, and action, by repeated use. We may be born with a tendency in a certain direction, or we may acquire tendencies by suggestions from others; such as the examples of those around us, suggestions from reading, listening to teachers. We are a bundle of mental habits. Each time we indulge in an undesirable thought or habit, the easier does it become to repeat that thought or action. And the oftener we give forth a certain desirable thought, or perform a desirable action, the easier does it become for us to repeat that thought or action. Mental scientists are in the habit of speaking of desirable thoughts or mental attitudes as "positive," and of the undesirable ones as "negative." There is a good reason for this. The mind instinctively recognizes certain things as good for the individual to which it belongs, and it clears the path for such thoughts, and interposes the least resistance to them. They have a much greater effect than an undesirable thought possesses, and one positive thought will counteract a number of negative thoughts. The best way to overcome undesirable or negative thoughts and feelings is to cultivate the positive ones. The positive thought is the strongest plant, and will in time starve out the negative one by withdrawing from it the nourishment necessary for its existence. Of course the negative thought will set up a vigorous resistance at first, for it is a fight for life with it. In the slang words of the time, it "sees its finish" if the positive thought is allowed to grow and develop; and, consequently, it makes things unpleasant for the individual until he has started well into the work of starving it out. Brain cells do not like to be laid on the shelf any more than does any other form of living energy, and they rebel and struggle until Chapter XII. Developing New Brain-Cells. 59 they become too weak to do so. The best way is to pay as little attention as possible to these weeds of the mind, but put in as much time as possible watering, caring for and attending to the new and beautiful plants in the garden of the mind. For instance, if you are apt to hate people, you can best overcome the negative thought by cultivating Love in its place. Think Love, and act it out, as often as possible. Cultivate thoughts of kindness, and act as kindly as you can to everyone with whom you come in contact. You will have trouble at the start, but gradually Love will master Hate, and the latter will begin to droop and wither. If you have a tendency toward the "blues" cultivate a smile, and a cheerful view of things. Insist upon your mouth wearing up-turned corners, and make an effort of the will to look upon the bright side of things. The "blue -devils" will set up a fight, of course, but pay no attention to them— just go on cultivating optimism and cheerfulness. Let "Bright, Cheerful and Happy," be your watchword, and try to live it out. These recipes may seem very old and timeworn, but they are psychological truths and may be used by you to advantage. If you once comprehend the nature of the thing, the affirmations and auto-suggestions of the several schools may be understood and taken advantage of. You may make yourself energetic instead of slothful, active instead of lazy, by this method. It is all a matter of practice and steady work. New Thought people often have much to say about "holding the thought;" and, indeed, it is necessary to "hold the thought" in order to accomplish results. But something more is needed. You must "act out" the thought until it becomes a fixed habit with you. Thoughts take form in action; and in turn actions influence thought. So by "acting out" certain lines of thought, the actions react upon the mind, and increase the development of the part of the mind having close relation to the act. Each time the mind entertains a thought, the easier becomes the resulting action— and each time an act is performed, the easier becomes the corresponding thought. So you see the thing works both ways—action and reaction. If you feel cheerful and happy, it is very natural for you to laugh. And if you will Thought Vibration 60 laugh a little, you will begin to feel bright and cheerful. Do you see what I am trying to get at? Here it is, in a nutshell: If you wish to cultivate a certain habit of action, begin by cultivating the mental attitude corresponding to it. And as a means of cultivating that mental attitude, start in to "act-out," or go through, the motions of the act corresponding to the thought. Now, see if you cannot apply this rule. Take up something that you really feel should be done, but which you do not feel like doing. Cultivate the thought leading up to it—say to yourself: "I like to do so and so," and then go through the motions (cheerfully, remember!) and act out the thought that you like to do the thing. Take an interest in the doing—study out the best way to do it—put brains into it—take a pride in it—and you will find yourself doing the thing with a considerable amount of pleasure and interest—you will have cultivated a new habit. If you prefer trying it on some mental trait of which you wish to be rid, it will work the same way. Start in to cultivate the opposite trait, and think it out and act it out for all you are worth. Then watch the change that will come over you. Don't be discouraged at the resistance you will encounter at first, but sing gaily: "I Can and I Will," and get to work in earnest. The important thing in this work is to keep cheerful and interested. If you manage to do this, the rest will be easy.

16

The Attractive Power—Desire Force.

Mental leaks—The man or woman in search of success—When Mental Force operates best—The Mind works on the sub-conscious plane along the line of the ruling passion or desire—Scattering thought- force—Getting out of the current of attraction—My personal experience—"Love" at the bottom of the whole of life—The so-called "chemical affinities"— Desire a manifestation of this Universal Life Love. We have discussed the necessity of getting rid of fear, that your desire may have full strength with which to work. Supposing that you have mastered this part of the task, or at least started on the road to mastery, I will now call your attention to another important branch of the subject. I allude to the subject of mental leaks. No, I don't mean the leakage arising from your failure to keep your own secrets—that is also important, but forms another story. The leakage I am now referring to is that occasioned by the habit of having the attention attracted to and distracted by every passing fancy. In order to attain a thing it is necessary that the mind should fall in love with it, and be conscious of its existence, almost to the exclusion of everything else. You must get in love with the thing you wish to attain, just as much as you would if you were to meet the girl or man you wished to marry. I do not mean that you should become a monomaniac upon the subject, Chapter XIII. The Attractive Power—Desire Force. 63 and should lose all interest in everything else in the world—that won't do, for the mind must have recreation and change. But, I do mean that you must be so "set" upon the desired thing that all else will seem of secondary importance. A man in love may be pleasant to everyone else, and may go through the duties and pleasures of life with good spirit, but underneath it all he is humming to himself "Just One Girl;" and every one of his actions is bent toward getting that girl, and making a comfortable home for her. Do you see what I mean? You must get in love with the thing you want, and you must get in love with it in earnest—none of this latter-day flirting, "on-today and off-tomorrow" sort of love, but the good old-fashioned kind, that used to make it impossible for a young man to get to sleep unless he took a walk around his best girl's house, just to be sure it was still there. That's the real kind! And the man or woman in search of success must make of that desired thing his ruling passion—he must keep his mind on the main chance. Success is jealous—that's why we speak of her as feminine. She demands a man's whole affection, and if he begins flirting with other fair charmers, she soon turns her back upon him. If a man allows his strong interest in the main chance to be sidetracked, he will be the loser. Mental Force operates best when it is concentrated. You must give to the desired thing your best and most earnest thought. Just as the man who is thoroughly in love will think out plans and schemes whereby he may please the fair one, so will the man who is in love with his work or business give it his best thought, and the result will be that a hundred and one plans will come into his field of consciousness, many of which are very important. The mind works on the subconscious plane, remember, and almost always along the lines of the ruling passion or desire. It will fix up things, and patch together plans and schemes, and when you need them the most it will pop them into your consciousness, and you will feel like hurrahing, just as if you had received some valuable aid from outside.

But if you scatter your thought-force, the subconscious mind will not know just how to please you, and the result is that you are apt to be put off from this source of aid and assistance. Beside this, you will miss the powerful result of concentrated thought in the conscious working out of the details of your plans. And then again the man whose mind is full of a dozen interests fails to exert the attracting power that is manifested by the man of the one ruling passion, and he fails to draw to him persons, things, and results that will aid in the working out of his plans, and will also fail to place himself in the current of attraction whereby he is brought into contact with those who will be glad to help him because of harmonious interests. I have noticed, in my own affairs, that when I would allow myself to be side-tracked by anything outside of my regular line of work, it would be only a short time before my receipts dropped off, and my business showed signs of a lack of vitality. Now, many may say that this was because I left undone some things that I would have done if my mind had been centered on the business. This is true; but I have noticed like results in cases where there was nothing to be done—cases in which the seed was sown, and the crop was awaited. And, in just such cases, as soon as I directed my thought to the matter the seed began to sprout. I do not mean that I had to send out great mental waves with the idea of affecting people—not a bit of it. I simply began to realize what a good thing I had, and how much people wanted it, and how glad they would be to know of it, and all that sort of thing, and lo! my thought seemed to vitalize the work, and the seed began to sprout. This is no mere fancy, for I have experienced it on several occasions; I have spoken to many others on the subject, and I find that our experiences tally perfectly. So don't get into the habit of permitting these mental leaks. Keep your Desire fresh and active, and let it get in its work without interference from conflicting desires. Keep in love with the thing you wish to attain—feed your fancy with it—see it as accomplished already, but don't lose your interest. Keep your eye on the main chance, and keep your one ruling passion strong Chapter XIII. The Attractive Power—Desire Force. 65 and vigorous. Don't be a mental polygamist—one mental love is all that a man needs—that is, one at a time. Some scientists have claimed that something that might as well be called "Love" is at the bottom of the whole of life. They claim that the love of the plant for water causes it to send forth its roots until the loved thing is found. They say that the love of the flower for the sun, causes it to grow away from the dark places, so that it may receive the light. The so-called "chemical affinities" are really a form of love. And Desire is a manifestation of this Universal Life Love. So I am not using a mere figure of speech when I tell you that you must love the thing you wish to attain. Nothing but intense love will enable you to surmount the many obstacles placed in your path. Nothing but that love will enable you to bear the burdens of the task. The more Desire you have for a thing, the more you Love it; and the more you Love it, the greater will be the attractive force exerted toward its attainment—both within yourself, and outside of you. So love but one thing at a time—don't be a mental Mormon.

17

The Great Dynamic Forces.

The difference between the successful strong men and the unsuccessful weak men—Energy and Invincible Determination—Energy not rare—Wasted nerve-force—The Human Will—A great dynamic force—The people who have "arrived"—Are they "ordinary," after all?—Made of the stuff of those about them—Wherein does their greatness lie?—Belief in themselves—The right use of material—The "trick" of greatness—The good things locked up in your mind—The inexhaustible supply. You have noticed the difference between the successful and strong men in any walk of life, and the unsuccessful weak men around them. You are conscious of the widely differing characteristics of the two classes, but somehow find it difficult to express just in what the difference lies. Let us take a look at the matter. Buxton said: "The longer I live, the more certain I am that the great difference between men, the feeble and the powerful, the great and the insignificant, is energy and invincible determination—a purpose once fixed and then Death or Victory. That quality will do anything that can be done in this world—and no talents, no circumstances, no opportunities will make a two- legged creature a man without it." I do not see how the idea could be more clearly expressed than Buxton has spoken. He has put his finger right in the center of the subject—his eye has seen into the heart of it. Energy and invincible determination—these two things will sweep away mighty barriers, and will surmount the greatest obstacles. And yet they must be used together. Energy without determination will go to waste. Lots of men have plenty of energy—they are full to overflowing with it; and yet they lack concentration—they lack the concentrated force that enables them to bring their power to bear upon the right spot. Energy is not nearly so rare a thing as many imagine it to be. I can look around me at any time, and pick out a number of people I know who are full of energy—many of them are energy plus—and yet, somehow, they do not seem to make any headway. They are wasting their energy all the time. Now they are fooling with this thing—now meddling with that. They will take up some trifling thing of no real interest or importance, and waste enough energy and nervous force to carry them through a hard day's work; and yet when they are through, nothing has been accomplished. Others who have plenty of energy, fail to direct it by the power of the Will toward the desired end. "Invincible determination"—those are the words. Do they not thrill you with their power? If you have something to do, get to work and do it. Marshal your energy, and then guide and direct it by your Will—bestow upon it that "invincible determination" and you will do the thing. Everyone has within him a giant will, but the majority of us are too lazy to use it. We cannot get ourselves nerved up to the point at which we can say, truthfully: "I Will." If we can but screw up our courage to that point, and will then pin it in place so that it will not slip back, we will be able to call into play that wonderful power—the Human Will. Man, as a rule, has but the faintest conception of the power of the Will, but those who have studied along the occult teachings, know that the Will is one of the great dynamic forces of the universe, and if harnessed and directed properly it is capable of accomplishing almost miraculous things. Thought Vibration 68 "Energy and Invincible Determination"—aren't they magnificent words? Commit them to memory—press them like a die into the wax of your mind, and they will be a constant inspiration to you in hours of need. If you can get these words to vibrating in your being, you will be a giant among pygmies. Say these words over and over again, and see how you are filled with new life—see how your blood will circulate—how your nerves will tingle. Make these words a part of yourself, and then go forth anew to the battle of life, encouraged and strengthened. Put them into practice. "Energy and Invincible Determination"—let that be your motto in your work-a-day life, and you will be one of those rare men who are able to "do things." Many persons are deterred from doing their best by the fact that they underrate themselves by comparison with the successful ones of life, or rather, overrate the successful ones by comparison with themselves. One of the curious things noticed by those who are brought in contact with the people who have "arrived" is the fact that these successful people are not extraordinary after all. You meet with some great writer, and you are disappointed to find him very ordinary indeed. He does not converse brilliantly, and, in fact, you know a score of everyday people who seem far more brilliant than this man who dazzles you by his brightness in his books. You meet some great statesman, and he does not seem nearly so wise as lots of old fellows in your own village, who waste their wisdom upon the desert air. You meet some great captain of industry, and he does not give you the impression of the shrewdness so marked in some little bargain-driving trader in your own town. How is this, anyway? Are the reputations of these people fictitious, or what is the trouble? The trouble is this: You have imagined these people to be made of superior metal, and are disappointed to find them made of the same stuff as yourself and those about you. But, you ask, wherein does their greatness of achievement lie? Chiefly in this: Belief in themselves and in their inherent power, in their faculty to concentrate on the work in hand, when they are working, and in their ability to prevent leaks of power when they are not working. They believe in themselves, and make every effort count. Your village wiseman spills his wisdom on every corner, and talks to a lot of fools; when if he really were wise he would save up his wisdom and place it where it would do some work. The brilliant writer does not waste his wit upon every comer; in fact, he shuts the drawer in which he contains his wit, and opens it only when he is ready to concentrate and get down to business. The captain of industry has no desire to impress you with his shrewdness and "smartness." He never did, even when he was young. While his companions were talking and boasting, and "blowing," this future successful financier was "sawin' wood and sayin' nuthin'." The great people of the world—that is, those who have "arrived"—are not very different from you, or me, or the rest of us—all of us are about the same at the base. You have only to meet them to see how very "ordinary" they are, after all. But, don't forget the fact that they know how to use the material that is in them; while the rest of the crowd does not, and, in fact, even doubts whether the true stuff is there. The man or woman who "gets there," usually starts out by realizing that he or she is not so very different, after all, from the successful people that they hear so much about. This gives them confidence, and the result is they find out that they are able to "do things." Then they learn to keep their mouths closed, and to avoid wasting and dissipating their energy. They store up energy, and concentrate it upon the task at hand; while their companions are scattering their energies in every direction, trying to show off and let people know how smart they are. The man or woman who "gets there," prefers to wait for the applause that follows deeds accomplished, and cares very little for the praise that attends promises of what we expect to do "some day," or an exhibition of "smartness" without works. One of the reasons that people who are thrown in with successful men often manifest success themselves, is that they are able to watch the successful man and sort of "catch the trick" of his greatness. They see that he is an everyday sort of man, but that he thoroughly believes in himself, and Thought Vibration 70 also that he does not waste energy, but reserves all his force for the actual tasks before him. And, profiting by example, they start to work and put the lesson into practice in their own lives. Now what is the moral of this talk? Simply this: Don't undervalue yourself, or overvalue others. Realize that you are made of good stuff, and that locked within your mind are many good things. Then get to work and unfold those good things, and make something out of that good stuff. Do this by attention to the things before you, and by giving to each the best that is in you, knowing that plenty of more good things are in you, ready for the fresh tasks that will come. Put the best of yourself into the undertaking on hand, and do not cheat the present task in favor of some future one. Your supply is inexhaustible. And don't waste your good stuff on the crowd of gapers, watchers and critics who are standing around watching you work. Save your good stuff for your job, and don't be in too much of a hurry for applause. Save up your good thoughts for "copy" if you are a writer; save up your bright schemes for actual practice, if you are a business man; save up your wisdom for occasion, if you are a statesman; and, in each case, avoid the desire to scatter your pearls before—well, before the gaping crowd that wants to be entertained by a "free show." Nothing very "high" about this teaching, perhaps, but it is what many of you need very much. Stop fooling, and get down to business. Stop wasting good raw material, and start to work making something worth while.

18

Claiming Your Own

Nothing too good for you—Your direct inheritance—Great things lost for want of asking— The Law takes you in earnest—You are a manifestation of the Whole Thing—You must first awaken to a realization that you are merely asking for "your own"—The Law will do its work—The hypnotism of "humility"—The great things in the Cosmos which await your coming of age—The playthings of life—Our game-tasks—The difference between the Master of Circumstances and the Slave of Circumstances. I n a recent conversation, I was telling a woman to pluck up courage and to reach out for a certain good thing for which she had been longing for many years, and which, at last, appeared to be in sight. I told her that it looked as if her desire was about to be gratified—that the Law of Attraction was bringing it to her. She lacked faith, and kept on repeating, "Oh! it's too good to be true—it's too good for me!" She had not emerged from the worm-of-the-dust stage, and although she was in sight of the Promised Land she refused to enter it because it "was too good for her." I think I succeeded in putting sufficient "ginger" into her to enable her to claim her own, for the last reports indicate that she is taking possession. But that is not what I wish to tell you. I want to call your attention to the fact that nothing is too good for you—no matter how great the thing may be—no matter how undeserving you may seem to be. You are entitled to the best there is, for it is your direct inheritance. So don't be afraid to ask— demand—and take. The good things of the world are not the portion of any favored sons. They belong to all, but they come only to those who are wise enough to recognize that the good things are theirs by right, and who are sufficiently courageous to reach out for them. Many good things are lost for want of the asking. Many splendid things are lost to you because of your feeling that you are unworthy of them. Many great things are lost to you because you lack the confidence and courage to demand and take possession of them. "None but the brave deserves the fair," says the old adage, and the rule is true in all lines of human effort. If you keep on repeating that you are unworthy of the good thing—that it is too good for you—the Law will be apt to take you at your word and believe what you say. That's a peculiar thing about the Law—it believes what you say—it takes you in earnest. So beware what you say to it, for it will be apt to give credence. Say to it that you are worthy of the best there is, and that there is nothing too good for you, and you will be likely to have the Law take you in earnest, and say, "I guess he is right; I'm going to give him the whole bakeshop if he wants it— he knows his rights, and what's the use of trying to deny it to him?" But if you say, "Oh, it's too good for me!" the Law will probably say, "Well, I wouldn't wonder but what that is so. Surely he ought to know, and it isn't for me to contradict him." And so it goes. Why should anything be too good for you? Did you ever stop to think just what you are? You are a manifestation of the Whole Thing, and have a perfect right to all there is. Or, if you prefer it this way, you are a child of the Infinite, and are heir to it all. You are telling the truth in either statement, or both. At any rate, no matter for what you ask, you are merely demanding your own. And the more in earnest you are about demanding it—the more confident you are of receiving it—the more will you use in reaching out for it—the surer you will be to obtain it.

Strong desire—confident expectation—courage in action—these things bring to you your own. But before you put these forces into effect, you must awaken to a realization that you are merely asking for your own, and not for something to which you have no right or claim. So long as there exists in your mind the last sneaking bit of doubt as to your right to the things you want, you will be setting up a resistance to the operation of the Law. You may demand as vigorously as you please, but you will lack the courage to act, if you have a lingering doubt of your right to the thing you want. If you persist in regarding the desired thing as if it belonged to another, instead of to yourself, you will be placing yourself in the position of the covetous or envious man, or even in the position of a tempted thief. In such a case your mind will revolt at proceeding with the work, for it instinctively will recoil from the idea of taking what is not your own—the mind is honest. But when you realize that the best the Universe holds belongs to you as a Divine Heir, and that there is enough for all without your robbing anyone else; then the friction is removed, and the barrier broken down, and the Law proceeds to do its work. I do not believe in this "humble" business. This meek and lowly attitude does not appeal to me—there is no sense in it, at all. The idea of making a virtue of such things, when Man is the heir of the Universe, and is entitled to whatever he needs for his growth, happiness and satisfaction! I do not mean that one should assume a blustering and domineering attitude of mind— that is also absurd, for true strength does not so exhibit itself. The blusterer is a self-confessed weakling—he blusters to disguise his weakness. The truly strong man is calm, self-contained, and carries with him a consciousness of strength which renders unnecessary the bluster and fuss of assumed strength. But get away from this hypnotism of "humility"—this "meek and lowly" attitude of mind. Remember the horrible example of Uriah Heep, and beware of imitating him. Throw back your head, and look the world square in the face. There's nothing to be afraid of—the world is apt to be as much afraid of you, as you are of it, anyway. Be a man, or woman, and not a crawling thing. And this applies to your mental attitude, as well as to your outward demeanor. Stop this crawling in your mind. See yourself as standing erect and facing life without fear, and you will gradually grow into your ideal. There is nothing that is too good for you—not a thing. The best there is, is not beginning to be good enough for you; for there are still better things ahead. The best gift that the world has to offer is a mere bauble compared to the great things in the Cosmos that await your coming of age. So don't be afraid to reach out for these playthings of life—these baubles of this plane of consciousness. Reach out for them—grab a whole fistful—play with them until you are tired; that's what they are made for, anyway. They are made for our express use—not to look at, but to be played with, if you desire. Help yourself—there's a whole shopful of these toys awaiting your desire, demand and taking. Don't be bashful! Don't let me hear any more of this silly talk about things being too good for you. Pshaw! You have been like the Emperor's little son thinking that the tin soldiers and toy drum were far too good for him, and refusing to reach out for them. But you don't find this trouble with children as a rule. They instinctively recognize that nothing is too good for them. They want all that is in sight to play with, and they seem to feel that the things are theirs by right. And that is the condition of mind that we seekers after the Divine Adventure must cultivate. Unless we become as little children we cannot enter the Kingdom of Heaven. The things we see around us are the playthings of the Kindergarten of God, playthings which we use in our game-tasks. Help yourself to them—ask for them without bashfulness—demand as many as you can make use of— they are yours. And if you don't see just what you want, ask for it—there's a big reserve stock on the shelves, and in the closets. Play, play, play, to your heart's content. Learn to weave mats—to build houses with the blocks—to stitch outlines on the squares—play the game through, and play it well. And demand all the proper materials for the play—don't be bashful—there's enough to go round. But-remember this! While all this be true, the best things are still only game-things—toys, blocks, mats, cubes, and all the rest. Useful, most useful for the learning of the lessons—pleasant, most pleasant with which to play— and desirable, most desirable, for these purposes. Get all the fun and profit out of the use of things that is possible. Throw yourself heartily into the game, and play it out—it is Good. But, here's the thing to remember—never lose sight of the fact that these good things are but playthings—part of the game—and you must be perfectly willing to lay them aside when the time comes to pass into the next class, and not cry and mourn because you must leave your playthings behind you. Do not allow yourself to become unduly attached to them—they are for your use and pleasure, but are not a part of you—not essential to your happiness in the next stage. Despise them not because of their lack of Reality—they are great things relatively, and you may as well have all the fun out of them that you can—don't be a spiritual prig, standing aside and refusing to join in the game. But do not tie yourself to them—they are good to use and play with, but not good enough to use you and to make you a plaything. Don't let the toys turn the tables on you. This is the difference between the Master of Circumstances and the Slave of Circumstances. The Slave thinks that these playthings are real, and that he is not good enough to have them. He gets only a few toys, because he is afraid to ask for more, and he misses most of the fun. And then, considering the toys to be real, and not realizing that there are plenty more where these came from, he attaches himself to the little trinkets that have come his way, and allows himself to be made a slave of them. He is afraid that they may be taken away from him, and he is afraid to toddle across the floor and help himself to the others. The Master knows that all are his for the asking. He demands that which he needs from day to day, and does not worry about overloading himself; for he knows that there are "lots more," and that he cannot be cheated out of them. He plays, and plays well, and has a good time in the play—and he learns his Kindergarten lessons in the playing. But he does not become too much attached to his toys. He is willing to fling away the worn-out one, and reach out for a new one. And when he is called into the next room for promotion, he drops on the floor the worn-out toys of the day, and with glistening eyes and confident attitude of mind, marches into the next room—into the Great Unknown—with a smile on his face. He is not afraid, for he hears the voice of the Teacher, and knows that she is there waiting for him—in that Great Next Room.

19

Law, Not Chance.

The Attractive Power of Thought—"A matter of luck"—A magnificent illustration of the Law of Attraction—A strong belief as efficacious as a strong wish—The man who "gets there"— The man who fails—No such thing as Chance—Law everywhere—Plan and purpose; cause and effect—The right vibrations—Getting into the current. Some time ago I was talking to a man about the Attractive Power of Thought. He said that he did not believe that Thought could attract anything to him, and that it was all a matter of luck. He had found, he said, that ill luck relentlessly pursued him, and that everything he touched went wrong. It always had, and always would, and he had grown to expect it. When he undertook a new thing he knew beforehand that it would go wrong and that no good would come of it. Oh, no! there wasn't anything in the theory of Attractive Thought, so far as he could see; it was all a matter of luck! This man failed to see that by his own confession he was giving a most convincing argument in favor of the Law of Attraction. He was testifying that he was always expecting things to go wrong, and that they always came about as he expected. He was a magnificent illustration of the Law of Attraction—but he didn't know it, and no argument seemed to make the matter clear to him. He was "up against it," and there was no way out of it—he always expected the ill luck, and every occurrence proved that he was right, and that the Mental Science position was all nonsense. There are many people who seem to think that the only way in which the Law of Attraction operates is when one wishes hard, strong and steady. They do not seem to realize that a strong belief is as efficacious as a strong wish. The successful man believes in himself and in his ultimate Success, and, paying no attention to little setbacks, stumbles, tumbles and slips, presses on eagerly to the goal, believing all the time that he will get there. His views and aims may alter as he progresses, and he may change his plans or have them changed for him, but all the time he knows in his heart that he will eventually "get there." He is not steadily wishing he may get there—he simply feels it and believes it, and thereby sets into operation the strongest forces known in the world of thought. The man who just as steadily believes he is going to fail will invariably fail. How could he help it? There is no special miracle about it. Everything he does, thinks and says is tinctured with the thought of failure. Other people catch his spirit, and fail to trust him or his ability, which occurrences he in turn sets down as but other exhibitions of his ill luck, instead of ascribing them to his belief and expectation of failure. He is suggesting failure to himself all the time, and he invariably takes on the effect of the autosuggestion. Then, again, he by his negative thoughts shuts up that portion of his mind from which should come the ideas and plans conducive to success and which do come to the man who is expecting success because he believes in it. A state of discouragement is not the one in which bright ideas come to us. It is only when we are enthused and hopeful that our minds work out the bright ideas which we may turn to account. Men instinctively feel the atmosphere of failure hovering around certain of their fellows, and on the other hand recognize something about others which leads them to say, when they hear of a temporary mishap befalling such a one; "Oh, he'll come out all right somehow—you can't down him." It is the atmosphere caused by the prevailing Mental Attitude. Clear up your Mental Atmosphere! There is no such thing as chance. Law maintains everywhere, and all that happens happens because of the operation of Law. You cannot name the simplest thing that ever occurred by chance—try it, and then run the thing down to a final analysis, and you will see it as the result of Law. It is as plain as mathematics. Plan and purpose; cause and effect. From the movements of worlds to the growth of the grain of mustard seed—all the result of Law. The fall of the stone down the mountain-side is not chance—forces which had been in operation for centuries caused it. And back of that cause were other causes, and so on until the Causeless Cause is reached. And Life is not the result of chance—the Law is here, too. The Law is in full operation whether you know it or not—whether you believe in it or not. You may be the ignorant object upon which the Law operates, and bring yourself all sorts of trouble because of your ignorance of or opposition to the Law. Or you may fall in with the operations of the Law—get into its current, as it were—and Life will seem a far different thing to you. You cannot get outside of the Law, by refusing to have anything to do with it. You are at liberty to oppose it and produce all the friction you wish to—it doesn't hurt the Law, and you may keep it up until you learn your lesson. The Law of Thought Attraction is one name for the Law, or rather for one manifestation of it. Again I say, your thoughts are real things. They go forth from you in all directions, combining with thoughts of like kind—opposing thoughts of a different character—forming combinations—going where they are attracted—flying away from thought centers opposing them. And your mind attracts the thoughts of others, which have been sent out by them consciously or unconsciously. But it attracts only those thoughts which are in harmony with its own. Like attracts like, and opposites repel opposites, in the world of thought. If you set your mind to the keynote of courage, confidence, strength and success, you attract to yourself thoughts of like nature; people of like nature; things that fit in the mental tune. Your prevailing thought or mood determines that which is to be drawn toward you—picks out your mental bedfellow. You are today setting into motion thought currents which will in time attract toward you thoughts, people and conditions in harmony with the predominant note of your thought. Your thought will mingle with that of others of like nature and mind, and you will be attracted toward each other, and will surely come together with a common purpose sooner or later, unless one or the other of you should change the current of his thoughts. Fall in with the operations of the Law. Make it a part of yourself. Get into its currents. Maintain your poise. Set your mind to the keynote of Courage, Confidence and Success. Get in touch with all the thoughts of that kind that are emanating every hour from hundreds of minds. Get the best that is to be had in the thought world. The best is there, so be satisfied with nothing less. Get into partnership with good minds. Get into the right vibrations. You must be tired of being tossed about by the operations of the Law—get into harmony with it.